2008
GOD'S FINAL WITNESS

Ronald Weinland

Front cover picture by
The Stocktrek Corp/Brand X Pictures/PictureQuest

the-end.com, inc., P.O. Box 14447, Cincinnati, OH 45250
Visit our Web site at **www.the-end.com**

Library of Congress Cataloging-in-Publication Data
Weinland, Ronald.
    2008 – God's Final Witness
    ISBN: 0-9753240-6-3 (hardcover)
    ISBN: 0-9753240-7-1 (softcover)

International Publishing and Distribution:

the-end.com, inc.
Post Office Box 4767, Knox City,
Wantirna South, VIC 3152
AUSTRALIA

the-end.com, inc.
Postbus 70
2900 SCHOTEN (Antwerpen),
BELGIE

2008
GOD'S FINAL WITNESS

Chapter 1

GOD'S TWO WITNESSES

It is with apprehension and heaviness of heart that I begin to write a second book. My first book, *The Prophesied End-Time*, was published nearly a year and a half ago and has been distributed in over 100 countries. It describes the prophetic end-time destruction that is about to come on this earth. It foretells of World War III and the overthrow of the United States, Canada, Australia, New Zealand, the United Kingdom, and much of Western Europe. Some of these events, as well as other prophesied conflicts, will now be covered in more detail; although these are not the primary focus of this book.

There are many fictional books and movies about apocalyptic events that result in massive destruction on earth. The source of such destruction is generally portrayed as man-made, the result of natural disasters, or sometimes, the result of invasion from beyond this earth. This NON-fiction book reveals a combination of all three sources, ending in massive destruction of most of this earth, including most of its population.

This is not easy to write; it will not be easy to read. You may not read past the first few pages before you decide that this is too outrageous to continue. Nevertheless, it is all true! And you owe it to yourself and those you love to fully consider what is written here.

Interviews

The publicist of my first book scheduled interviews for me throughout the United States. Those interviews began in September 2004. I mention this because there was an underlying theme that ran throughout those interviews which will help you to better understand the need for this second book. Final end-time events that will lead into the great tribulation, at the opening of the Seventh Seal, have already begun. These were covered in *The Prophesied End-Time*, as well as the interviews.

Understandably, it was difficult for the hosts of those interviews to believe that this world is about to enter a time of destruction which will ultimately end 6,000 years of man's government—man's self-rule. One of the most common questions or sentiment was, "Why should anyone believe you over so many others who, throughout time, have made predictions about the end-time or the end of this world?" The answer is twofold and was partially addressed in the first book.

Before the first answer is given, it should be noted that toward the end of the interviews, one phase of end-time events was well under way. (Many of those interviews can be heard on a website to be given later in this chapter.)

In December of 2004, a great tsunami, originating in the Indian Ocean, struck several countries with massive destruction and a death toll that has been estimated at well over 225,000. The UN estimated the number of people displaced by the tsunami to be five million. This tsunami, caused by an earthquake, is the second strongest in recorded history. It has been followed by an escalation in the number and magnitude of earthquakes worldwide.

The United States witnessed a record breaking year for hurricanes both in number and magnitude. 2005 had the most named tropical storms on record. Letters of the Greek Alphabet have never been used to name storms, but even now in December, Hurricane Epsilon has become the fifth named storm in the Greek Alphabet. This past year witnessed the highest number of hurricanes on record along with the most category five storms ever. In August, Hurricane Katrina produced the greatest destruction from a natural disaster ever seen in the U.S., which left some areas of New Orleans almost wiped out. This devastation is so great that there is not enough time to rebuild it before this age of man comes to an end.

From another perspective, the average number of named storms in any season is 10, but in 2005 there were 26. The average number of hurricanes is 6, but 2005 had 14. The average number of major hurricanes is 2, but 2005 had 7.

Then, in October, a massive earthquake struck northern Pakistan with collateral destruction extending into India. As a result, over 80,000 people lost their lives and approximately 2.5 million were left homeless.

But before these disasters occurred, many of the interview hosts questioned the validity of what was written in *The Prophesied End-Time*. In those interviews, they were told that such events would begin to occur and continue to increase in magnitude over the following four years. But the question was asked, "Haven't there always been earthquakes and other destructive forces that have claimed large numbers of lives?" The answer is yes, but the whole point of this is the answer to the question, "Why should anyone believe all this?"

These events are occurring exactly as these books describe. Yes, through time, natural disasters have resulted in great destruction and loss of life. The difference is, that now, we are at the beginning of the final events which will culminate in the end of this age—the end of man's self-rule on earth.

The proof of the validity of my first book, and now this one, is in the timing and the destruction that follows, exactly as both books describe.

God gives the analogy of a woman in labor pain to show how these events will unfold. As labor begins, the contractions are farther apart and less intense; but as time between contractions decreases, the intensity of those contractions grows. Such is the reality of labor pain, and such will be part of the proof of what is written here.

What we have witnessed since those interviews a year ago will only increase in magnitude and frequency until we come to the last and final stage. This final stage is referred to as the great tribulation which is prophesied to last for a final three and one-half years. It will begin with one-third of the United States being destroyed—followed by World War III.

So what makes what I have to say in these two books any different from what others have had to say about the end-time? You need to ask, "Who else has laid everything on the line, and in such detail, as found in these two books?"

Over the centuries, people have seen natural disasters and predicted that man was in the end-times of Bible prophecy. But throughout time, they have been wrong. The Bible has much to say about such times, therefore, it has been a natural consequence that these "religious" people have made such predictions. The difference is that **now** it is true! We have now entered the end-times.

Today, people are making the same kind of claims as others have done for centuries; but this time they just "happen" to be right that this is the end. Due to the magnitude of the disastrous events that have occurred over the past year, there has been a marked increase in popularity and interest in end-time predictions and the growing willingness of "religious types" to make more pronouncements. But all of them are wrong in their conclusions, except for one coincidental truth—this **is** the end-time.

Such prognosticators will only increase as disastrous events increase, and they will deceive many people. It is easy to "jump on the band wagon" (an American expression used to describe the behavior of conformists and opportunists). As disastrous events increase, they will claim that each event is some kind of sign or that it has special religious significance—**after** the event has already occurred. But who is presenting a time frame and getting more specific as all this increases? Who is putting all this together so that people can understand what is happening and why, while also informing people of what is coming upon the United States once the Seventh Seal of the Book of Revelation has been opened?

An example of some obnoxious religious opportunists concerns some who have made claims that New Orleans was devastated by the hurricane because of God's punishment for her sinful ways. And yet others say it was God's punishment on the U.S. for occupying Iraq. Still others conclude it was a specific sign that we are entering the end-times. All of these people are religious opportunists who are no different from those of ages gone by.

The claim that what happened to New Orleans was "a sign," is closest to being true; but it is still wrong. The tragedy of New Orleans is not a specific sign; it is only part of an overall sign of a "woman in labor." The devastation of New Orleans is not a Biblical sign of itself, and it is not mentioned by God as a single sign of the end-time.

The sign of a woman in labor involves numerous natural disasters and acts of terrorism that will continue to increase in magnitude and intensity. These are not significant individually, but they are cumulatively! Specific events will follow all this, and many of these events will be described more thoroughly in later chapters. The first, which has already been mentioned in part, is the destruction of one-third of the United States.

The Answer

Again, the underlying current of the interviewers was, "Why should anyone believe you over others?" So indeed, why should anyone believe what is written in either book?

That is the whole point! People cannot believe these things unless there is proof. This is part of the reason God has chosen to reveal end-time events in the manner that He has. Through the centuries, people have been lied to about God; this very subject will be covered in the next chapter. **Every** religion in this world cannot be right about God. All of them can't be true. The very definition of "truth" cries out that only one thing can be true. Only one way can be God's way. This is a great dilemma for man.

If the Catholics are right in what they teach, then all the Protestant churches are wrong. If a particular Protestant group is right, then the Catholics are wrong, and so is every other Protestant group. If Judaism is true, then all Christianity is false. If Islam is true, then Judaism and Christianity are false. Only **one way** and **one truth** can be genuine! Do you see the dilemma?

If the Pharisees were right, in the time of Christ, then the Sadducees were wrong, and vise-versa. But Jesus Christ made it clear that both of them were wrong!

Only God can make the truth prevail. We are at the very time when God is doing exactly that! After 6,000 years, God is in the process of bringing the world into one order, away from the control of man's self-rule. Through the process of end-time events, God is bringing the world under one government, with only one true religion. God proclaims that this new world government will last for 1,000 years, with even greater changes beyond that.

As I told the interviewers, I do not expect anyone to believe this yet. In a very few years, more and more people will begin to believe what God is doing, and what He is allowing to occur on earth. The change from one world to another will not come easily. It is likened to a woman in labor before delivering her child. People will begin to change the way they think throughout the end-time because they will see the proof of God unfold before their very eyes. This book reveals that proof; **time** unveils it!

God is beginning to make a distinction between what is His truth and all that is false in the world. When all of it is finished, only the truth will prevail; and, all lies and liars will have been exposed.

So the answer is that most do not believe and cannot; but all who survive will eventually believe what God says concerning this end-time, because in time, all that is true will be revealed—and in a very short time at that. As described in my first book, most will resist what is true and most will resist to the point of death. The truth is, that eventually, in the United States alone, over 250 million will die. Your hope for survival will depend largely upon your response to the truth when God begins to reveal who He is and who He is not. Only by responding to God and turning to Him "in the truth" can you hope for His mercy and intervention to give you aid.

So what will you do as world conditions worsen and catastrophic events unfold with greater intensity and frequency? The day is fast approaching when you will cry out for answers! You can begin to receive those answers now.

A Twofold Answer

Why should anyone believe what is written in either book? Again, the answer is twofold. The answer is not in anything that is stated or written because words by themselves do not prove credibility and truth. That which man has written about God does not prove it is true. Only God Himself can prove what is true by bringing to pass exactly what He has said. Only the next few years can prove whether or not these two books are true and of God. If nothing happens, then you can know positively that this is complete fiction. However, if things continue to happen as described, then you have much to fear! And indeed, man has much to fear because God has declared that we are now entering the most catastrophic time of all human history. The God of Abraham declares that there has never been a time like this one coming, and there never will be one like it again.

So again, the first answer is that people are not able to believe what is written until they begin to admit the growing evidence of a woman in labor—that devastation is increasing in magnitude and frequency. Only then can people really begin to believe what they are witnessing. This is one of the main reasons these books have been written, so that people can begin to respond to the one Great Creator God when they see these things come to pass.

The second part of this twofold answer will come in a similar manner. People will begin to believe what is written as God begins to reveal more powerfully what is true through His two end-time witnesses—His two prophets for the end-time. This book and this very chapter are written to announce the beginning of that revelation from God.

These two witnesses of God, as recorded in the Book of Revelation, will do their work during the last three and one-half years of their lives, which is the same time period as the great and final tribulation that will come on the entire world. This period of time will begin with one-third of the United States being destroyed! More about this will be addressed later.

The stories of the Bible are recorded as being true, but that does not mean people believe them; these two books tell the truth, but that does not mean people will believe them. The overwhelming majority of those who have read the first book do not yet believe what is written in it. Some people believe part of it, while others have adopted a "wait and see" approach. This is fully understandable because they need proof. God is going to give them **great** proof.

How many people today actually believe the story of Noah's flood? Many so-called religious scholars don't even believe it actually happened. They think it is a "nice story" containing symbolism that can teach valuable lessons. Why don't people believe it? Their response is, "Where is the proof?" Believing the account of the flood is strictly a matter of faith because there is no strong physical evidence. Therefore, most people do not believe in a literal flood.

If you had lived in the time of Noah, you would have been a believer. Ultimately, everyone in the world at that time believed what God said through Noah. It took him and his family 120 years to build the ark. Very few people believe that such a ship could be built by a single family, over such a period of time, and hold the number of animals described; but those who lived at that time and in that area saw this project. Eventually, as everyone witnessed the rising waters, they began to believe what God said through Noah.

So much of what is written in the Bible is received by people in this manner. People want proof; they want powerful proof! So God is going to give just that—a final witness to mankind.

We have entered the end-time. As with the time of Noah, we can say that the rains have begun, and soon, the water will begin to rise. End-time events will become far more devastating, growing in frequency, until we are finally thrown into the midst of the water when the final three and one-half years of great tribulation strike.

God's Two End-Time Witnesses

Throughout the history of man's 6,000 years on earth, God sent His prophets to tell mankind about His ways and the need to repent of their ways and turn to Him. But man is filled with such pride and self-will that, for the most part, he has not listened to God or turned to His ways. Only a very, very few through time have listened.

The overall history of man is that he will not listen to God. Knowing that man will not listen to Him, God sent his prophets, not only to tell people to turn to Him (repent of their ways), but that disobedience to their Creator would have consequences. God sent prophets with specific messages about what would happen to them if they did not listen.

For six millennia, God has been patient toward man's unwillingness to listen to Him through His prophets. This has much to do with why God is once again—one last time—sending His prophets (His two witnesses) into the world in the most powerful way yet.

The early Church had some prophets, but they were sent to the Church and not the world. John, who wrote the Book of

Revelation, was not sent to the world with the prophecies he wrote. Jesus Christ is the Prophet of God spoken of in scripture, and certainly, as the Son of God, there is none other like Him. As for the other prophets among men, one must go back more than 2,500 years to find those whom God worked through in a great way. Yet, of all the major and minor prophets of the Old Testament, you will find that most were sent to the nation of Judah or Israel (or both), but they were not sent to the world.

One of the most notable times when God gave great power to a prophet was just over 3,000 years ago when He raised up Moses to lead the Israelites out of Egypt. This time marked the beginning of a new phase in God's plan—to work with a physical nation. At that time, God chose to begin revealing Himself to part of mankind in a greater way than ever before.

It is important to understand the story of Moses so that you can grasp the magnitude of what God will do through His end-time prophets. These two prophets will be sent into the world! In actuality, there has never been a time when God has given such power to His prophets to accomplish so much, and on a worldwide scale. These two witnesses will be the most formidable prophets God has ever used in all 6,000 years of human history.

Moses was understandably concerned that the Israelites would not believe him, so he asked God, "Who shall I tell them has sent me unto them?" God simply responded, "Tell them I AM has sent me unto you." But God also told Moses to tell the Israelites even more, instructing him to say, *"This is what you shall say to the children of Israel, 'The ETERNAL God of your fathers, the God of Abraham, the God of Isaac, and the God of Jacob, has sent me unto you'"* (Exodus 3:15).

Moses was to address the Israelites, and even Pharaoh, in a straightforward, matter-of-fact manner. It was not Moses' responsibility to try to prove this in some way; it was God's. God showed the Israelites and Egypt that Moses was His servant and His prophet by fulfilling what He said through him.

You should note that God did not use the gift of healing or the performance of other miraculous signs to deliver the Israelites from Egypt, and He will not use such signs in the end-time to reveal where He is working and with whom. Some people believe that God will perform such signs in the end-time to reveal His Church and His true servants. That is not true. Just as God humbled Israel and Egypt in Moses' day, He will do the same during the end-time. The whole world will be humbled before the power of Almighty God.

This miracle of God, the exodus of a nation of people from Egypt, sent fear throughout the world. God will once again show unrepentant mankind the consequences of opposing Him. The Almighty God is going to bring about the end of 6,000 years of man's self-rule on earth.

What God did through Moses is small by comparison to what He will do through His two end-time prophets—referred to as His two witnesses. Hopefully, you will begin to see the magnitude of what is being said in this book and what is about to come.

Importance of Two Witnesses

God is going to magnify His two end-time prophets in a way that He has never magnified His prophets before. Approximately one-third of the Bible contains prophecy from God, and nearly 80 percent of that prophecy applies to this end-time.

The major work of these two prophets will be during the last three and one-half years of this end-time—the most momentous time in all human history. This final period will be the culmination in God's plan of salvation, reaching a pinnacle, through this transition, from one age into another. When this period is over, the result will be good news for this earth and all mankind. However, the transitional period will be horrifying!

The majority of prophecies given by the prophets of old, including those given by Jesus Christ, are for our time now. Early prophets were not to witness the fulfillment of these end-time prophecies. Moses, King David, Isaiah, Jeremiah, and Ezekiel did not see these prophecies fulfilled. Even Daniel, to whom God gave very specific prophecy concerning the end-time, did not see these prophecies fulfilled.

After Daniel wrote the prophecies God gave him, he asked God about their meaning. Notice what God told Daniel about what he had written, *"And He said, 'Go your way Daniel because these words are closed up and sealed **until** the end-time"* (Daniel 12:9).

This time in all human history is so important because these prophecies pertain to our time now. It is at this time that God will accomplish the fulfillment of all the things written by all His prophets of old. This too is why God places so much importance on the revelation and work of His two end-time prophets. These two people will reveal the present-day meaning of all the end-time prophecies, and they will witness the fulfillment of all the writings of the prophets of old.

The work of these two prophets will be powerful and mighty before God. They will be instrumental in revealing God and His truth to this earth with power and strength on a scale that mankind has never witnessed in ages past. These two witnesses will proclaim the meaning of prophecies that have been hidden from man—prophecies that occupy over 25 percent of the Bible. They will give testimony (witness) of the validity of God's word that is to be revealed to man over the next few years. Then they will also witness their fulfillment, as will the rest of the world.

How important are these two witnesses to God's plan? What kind of significance does God place on them and their role? This can be answered in part by understanding some of the symbolism God gives concerning them.

God the Father and Jesus Christ inspired the prophet John to write the Book of Revelation. John never saw the fulfillment of what he wrote because it was not about his time. The beginning of Revelation is mostly about the Church of God that would continue for nearly 2,000 years, leading into the very end-time. John gave testimony about seven Church eras that would exist through this time. One era would follow another until the last era, the Laodicea era. The Church is in that era now, and near the end of it. Laodicea is the last era of the Church before the return of Jesus Christ as King of kings to rule the earth in God's government. Man's government is about to be brought to a close.

In the first chapter of Revelation, John describes these seven Church eras, in symbolism, as seven golden lamp stands. Certainly this symbolism is important to God because it is about His Church that has continued since the day of Pentecost in 31 A.D., with each era leading into the next, until the end. The next two chapters go on to describe the unique characteristics and role that each era would fulfill.

Later, in the Book of Revelation, God gives more symbolism that reflects the importance of His two witnesses. Notice what God says:

> *And I will give power unto my two witnesses, and they shall prophesy a thousand two hundred and sixty days, clothed in sackcloth* [symbolic of humility]. *These are the two olive trees, and the two lamp stands <u>standing</u>* [Gk.—set,

established] *before* [Gk.—in the presence of] *the God of the earth.* (Revelation 11:3-4)

A literal translation of this last verse is saying, "These are the two olive trees and the two lamp stands which are established in the presence of God unto the earth." These two people are represented as two lamp stands and two olive trees, which God sets before Him to reveal His will to the whole earth.

This symbolism is of great importance to God. It represents what He is about to accomplish on the earth through His two end-time prophets. The symbolism of the Church and these two witnesses is also recorded in Zechariah. This prophecy in Zechariah places great importance on the symbolism of the lamp stands that concerns the Church and the olive trees that represent God's two witnesses.

Zechariah was awakened out of a sleep by an angel and asked what he had seen.

> *I have looked, and behold a lamp stand all of gold, with a bowl upon the top of it, and its seven lamps thereon and seven pipes to the seven lamps, which are upon the top of it, and two olive trees by it, with one upon the right side of the bowl and the other upon the left side of it.* (Zechariah 4:2-3)

This is the same symbolism that was given to John concerning the Church eras and the two witnesses. Zechariah continued to question the angel:

> *What are these two olive trees upon the right side of the candle stand and upon the left side thereof? And I asked further and said to him, "What are these two olive branches which go through the two golden pipes to empty the golden oil out of themselves?" And he answered*

me and said, "Don't you know what these are?" And I
said, "No, my lord." Then he said, "These are the two
anointed ones that stand before the Lord unto the
whole earth." (Zechariah 4:11-14)

This prophecy in Zechariah is the same as what is clarified
more fully through John in the Book of Revelation. These two
olive trees that stand beside the candle stands, which picture the
seven Church eras, symbolize the importance, magnitude and
power that will conclude nearly 2,000 years of Church history
and 6,000 years of man's self-rule. God's two anointed ones,
His two witnesses—His two prophets, are established to witness
to the whole world about the greatest phase yet of His plan and
purpose for mankind. It is the prophetic transition from one era
to another, from man's self-rule to God's rule, from the
firstfruits of God's Church to the manifestation of the Kingdom
of God.

The Next Step

It is now with boldness, confidence and great clarity that I give to
you what God has given me. I am to announce, through God's
direct revelation, that I am one of those two witnesses. The other
witness will be revealed to the world during the time of the great
tribulation—within the final three and one-half years of man's era.
During that period of time, we will, together, completely fulfill all
that God has given us to witness to this whole earth. Then, at the
end, we will die in the streets of Jerusalem; and finally, exactly
three and one-half days later, we will be resurrected (Revelation
11). The world will see this resurrection via television. At this
same time Jesus Christ will appear in the heavens above the earth
as He is returning to take the reigns of man's government on earth.
All this will be explained more fully later in this book.

It is not my job to prove this to anyone—it is God's! He will do so by His great power. This is all about God—His plan, His purpose, His will, His judgment, His way, and His truth. My job is to tell it like it is—as God directs me.

I am to say as Moses said, "I AM has sent me to you." Yes, the ETERNAL God, the God of Abraham has sent me to you. I am to state clearly that I am an end-time prophet, a prophet of the God of Abraham.

A prophet of the God of Abraham is specifically given for a great purpose, which is to make clear that this book is not slanted to show favoritism to Judaism, Christianity or Islam, but to take all three back to a time of common ground. First and foremost, God will address the followers of those three religions. The rest of humanity will be dealt with differently.

There is only one true, eternal-living God. He created all the universe and man upon the earth. He is the God of Abraham. Yet, after Abraham, and on through time, religious ideas about God became horribly varied and obscure. Various offshoots began to believe that they were the only true religion and the only authentic representatives of God's Word.

God will now begin to reveal, and very powerfully, what is true and what is from Him. God will expose all that is false and not of Him.

People are not accustomed to hearing a prophet because no prophet has been sent by God during this generation, until now. No writings of a prophet have been recorded for centuries, until now. People are not accustomed to being spoken to in the way I am doing in this book. God will not cajole, plead or seek to be diplomatic with the feelings, beliefs or concerns of others. You are the one who must come into subjection to God. His ways will reign. All who resist and oppose God will be broken. The fragile sensitivities of the politically correct are of no concern to God.

This is not a time to test God. This is not a time to ignore God's words. This is not a time to "wait and see," although most will do so for as long as they can. This is not a time to hold onto your "religious" beliefs. This is all deeply true because this is the time that God has chosen to change the earth. This is the time He has chosen to remove all governments and religions. The time of man has come to an end. The time of God has come—it is NOW!

It all depends upon you. Catastrophic end-time events will be fulfilled. You can respond to God in a genuine manner, through repentance, and place yourself at His mercy seat, for Almighty God is a God of love. He is compassionate and full of mercy toward those who seek His ways. All other ways cause suffering, pain and oppression in life. God's desire is that we be free from all that, and this just happens to be the age of man when such deliverance is coming. As God delivered Israel from the burdens of Egypt, He is now going to deliver this entire world from the burdens of man's self-rule and the way of bondage that has come from Satan. However, this time, God is going to do all this on a scale that is many times greater.

Much to Consider

As God's prophetic writings unfold through their systematic unveiling and literal manifestation, the world will be confounded. You have much to ponder and consider as you read. Much of this will seem surreal, but it will be reality.

Radio interviews, regarding the first book, *The Prophesied End-Time*, reflect much about the attitude and nature of man. How could anyone seriously believe all that was written in it?

The world has been flooded with books that contain everything that man can imagine. Whatever subject interests you, something has been written about it. Is it any wonder that man is so skeptical? Is it any wonder that man is so confused, especially when it comes to so many different ideas—so much contradiction about God?

Future interviews, after the publication of this book, will take on an even stronger message; and they will be followed by greater end-time events. God is going to broadcast powerfully the message contained in both books. It is like the proverbial mustard seed, which starts out small but grows very large. Not very many copies of this book will go out into the world, but the book's message will go out; and it will become stronger as cataclysmic events in the world become stronger.

Man's ability to destroy himself will, itself, be destroyed. Man's oppression of man will be brought to an end. A world of unprecedented peace will follow. Can you imagine a world with no wars and no oppression, a world where people and businesses cooperate rather than compete, a world with one religion, a world with one government, and a world where everyone in government deals in righteousness rather than politics and selfish gain? This is the good news beyond all that is bad, which must first befall the earth. God speed that time!

A Final Matter

Some of the interviews, along with numerous call-in responses, addressed a question that needs to be answered here. Their concern referred to the timing of the end-time. This was approached in different ways, but basically it was stated as follows, "Isn't it true that no man knows the time or hour of these things?"

Again, this was stated in many different ways. Some were closer to the actual Biblical statements than others, but most stated this as a simple generality. This may have been addressed by some in a sincere manner, but most were "making a statement." Those who were making a statement were doing so in order to discredit me as a prophet. After all, if I contradict God's word, then how can I be a prophet? This would be true if they actually understood the Biblical statements to which they were referring.

They were referring to the occasion when Jesus Christ was with his disciples walking in the area of the temple and admiring the work. Jesus Christ then spoke of a time when the temple would be cast down and not one stone would be left upon another. He was not referring to the physical temple, which was later destroyed, but he was referring to the spiritual temple—the Church that would be cast down in the end-time.

The disciples responded to Christ's statements by asking him a question, *"And as he* [Jesus Christ] *sat upon the Mount of Olives, the disciples came unto him privately, saying, 'Tell us, when shall these things be and what shall be the sign of your coming, and of the end of the age?'"* (Matthew 24:3). This is often translated as "the end of the world." It is not the end of the world, but the end of an age—the age of man [his first 6,000 years on earth].

Jesus answered by giving them prophecies concerning the end-time, most of which applied to those things that would transpire in God's own Church. They would also parallel events that would occur in the world, bearing physical similarities, yet not the same. Much of this story is addressed more fully in *The Prophesied End-Time.*

After those prophecies were given by Jesus Christ, he went on to say, *"But no man knows that day or hour. No, not even the angels in heaven. But only the Father knows"* (Matthew 24:36). The same account in the Book of Mark adds, *"No man knows that day or hour. No, not the angels in heaven and not even the Son. Only the Father knows"* (Mark 13:32).

So the answer to the disciples was that the timing was only known by God the Father. This does not mean that God would not reveal the timing of events at a later time. These prophecies of Jesus Christ, concerning the signs of the end of the age, show that in time, they would become apparent, at least to those whom God would reveal them. Even the parallel prophecies given to John in the Book of Revelation show that the Seals of Revelation would one day have to be opened. As covered in the first book, those Seals are being opened by Jesus Christ. Therefore, the time to begin opening them has already been given to the Son by His Father.

As was also covered in the first book, the Seventh Seal, at the time of this writing, has not yet been opened. When that seal is opened, you can rest assured, the final tribulation has arrived. God says that time will last for three and one-half years. Prophecy shows that one-third of the United States will be destroyed after this seal is opened.

In addition, at the very end-time, God will give His two witnesses great power to accomplish the work He has for them to do. These two (and others who know them) know exactly the day when Jesus Christ will return. These two will know positively when God gives them this power, and from that time they know that exactly three and one-half years remain.

Notice: *"And I will give power unto my two witnesses, and they shall prophesy a thousand two hundred and sixty days, clothed in sackcloth"* (Revelation 11:3). The symbolism of "sackcloth" is given because these two will be filled with humility. That which they have been given to do is not about themselves, but about God and His plan being unveiled. They will not take credit to themselves, and they will not be lifted up with pride as a result of the focus placed upon them.

So this verse clearly shows that these two anointed ones of God have a specific time to do the primary thrust of their work. They know the exact day that Jesus Christ will return because they know their final work will last exactly 1,260 days. It is exactly at this point that they will be killed:

> *And when they* [the two witnesses] *shall have finished their testimony, the beast that ascends out of the bottomless pit* [Satan through his influence on men] *shall make war against them, and shall overcome them, and kill them. And their dead bodies shall lie in the street of the great city, which spiritually is called Sodom and Egypt, where also our Lord was crucified* [in Jerusalem]. *And they of the people and kindreds and tongues and nations shall see their dead bodies three and one-half days* [via television], *and their dead bodies shall not be allowed to be put in graves.* (Revelation 11:7-9)

These two prophets of God will complete the work that God has given them to do, then they will be killed in the streets of Jerusalem. Their bodies will remain in the streets of Jerusalem for three and one-half days while the world watches via television.

Then the unbelievable will happen. Many in the world, who still will not believe they are whom they say they are, will receive a very rude awakening. After all, if they remain dead beyond three and one-half days, then they cannot be of God.

After three and one-half days the Spirit of life from God entered into them [the two witnesses] *and they stood upon their feet. Then great fear fell upon them which saw them. And they heard a great voice from heaven saying unto them, "Come up here." And they ascended up to heaven in a cloud and their enemies saw this happening to them.* (Revelation 11:11-12)

These two prophets of God are resurrected from the dead, in the sight of all who are watching, and rise up into the heavens of the atmosphere of this earth. It is in this same time-frame that a massive resurrection of 144,000 also rise to meet Jesus Christ. The 144,000 will return with Christ on this same day after the seven last plagues are poured out upon the earth. It is at the beginning of this same day that the return of Jesus Christ becomes visible to the whole world.

Again, this is all quite basic because, by the time the Seventh Seal is opened, Jesus Christ most assuredly knows the day He will return to the earth the second time to take control of all government on earth. At what point the Father made known the timing to Jesus Christ, we do not know, but we do know that when the Seventh Seal is opened there will be three and one-half years until the return of Christ. The final work of the two witnesses will begin at the same time the Seventh Seal is opened, therefore, they will know the exact day of Christ's return.

Yes, I do know the timing of events as the Seals of Revelation are opening. I do know we are in the end-time and that six Seals have already been opened. I know the exact day the First Seal was opened. As will be covered in another chapter, I know the exact day the Sixth Seal was opened, and the world will be shocked and in horror on the day that the Seventh Seal is opened.

God has given to Jesus Christ the timing for the seals to be opened, and Jesus Christ, in turn, has given the timing to me. Those who will receive these words can receive the same. If people choose to remain ignorant, refusing God's word, then they will have to suffer for their arrogance and pride against God. Arrogance and pride are exactly what God is going to break in man. These resist God's way of peace and genuine love that man **should be expressing** toward God and one another.

Often, in a futile attempt to discredit what they do not understand concerning the timing for end-time events, some will quote the words of Jesus Christ, "No man knows that day or hour." Up until only a decade ago, this was still very true, but conditions and circumstances have now changed. The countdown for the end-time has already begun, and it began when Jesus Christ started to open the seals of Revelation, the first of which was opened on December 17, 1994.

Indeed, the skepticism in those interviews about *The Prophesied End-Time* is understandable. However, God is going to begin removing the skepticism of the world, especially once the Seventh Seal is opened. You can listen to those interviews on the following website: www.the-end.com.

Today, people are not accustomed to how God works through His prophets. They don't understand the reasons why, but you can be certain of one thing, *"The Lord GOD does nothing without revealing His secret to His servants the prophets"* (Amos 3:7).

Chapter 2

THE DECEPTION IN MAN

One of the most difficult things for people to do is admit they are wrong. Human nature tends to see itself as being right. We hold to our opinions and beliefs on nearly every subject as though we are right, and all others who are in disagreement are simply wrong. Think about it. Isn't that the way we are?

It doesn't matter where you turn or what you address, you constantly see people with different opinions at odds with each other.

God tells us that "*every way of a man is right in his own eyes*" (Proverbs 21:2). It is the way of human nature, yet God also tells man that only He can reveal the true motives of the heart—the mind of human nature. But who is really concerned about what God has to say? Man has always been determined to live his life his own way—the way that he sees fit, and as he does this, he considers himself to be right in his choices and decisions. But this is a lie, because the very core and inner working of human nature is based on pride and selfishness—self being first.

Whether man likes it or not, this base nature is the cause of the problems we experience. It is the cause of conflicts, arguments, dissension, envy, competition, hatred, wars, stress, and unhappiness in life. Herbert W. Armstrong, a wise man of God and an apostle in the twentieth century, taught millions that there are two basic ways of life. One is *give*, and one is *get*.

Man, by nature, lives the way of *get*. Only when people begin to seek God's help to change their nature can they begin to find the true ways to peace. Man simply does not know the way of peace. This is evidenced in a bloodstained earth through 6,000 years of human history.

A painful reality of life is to learn that the way of man is steeped in deception and lies. This truth has had a negative impact on human life far greater than most know or can admit.

We live life with many prejudices. Prejudices are hard to see in ourselves, and we have great difficulty admitting them. These prejudices have much to do with our own selfishness—our own self-interest—our own private corner of the world. What is your gender, nationality, race, or political persuasion? Do you have any bias on these subjects? Everyone has bias to address in his or her life. Facing your bias will help you learn much about yourself, but many simply cannot be truthful with themselves.

This leads us to address one of the most passionate subjects of all. It is the cause of the greatest division, hatred and deception on earth. It is religion!

Throughout time, this world's religions have been the greatest cause of evil and human suffering. You need to understand why!

One of the harshest realities people can face is to learn that they have been lied to about their religious beliefs—that they have been deceived. This is one of the most difficult barriers in life to break. People instinctively defend their beliefs because they are foundational to their entire outlook on life—the core of their decision-making process in all matters of life.

Lying—deception—is one of the most refined character flaws of mankind. Before we launch into more of what is about to happen on this earth and how God is going to overthrow all the governments of mankind, you need to preface your reading with some very basic knowledge.

Lies, Lies and More Lies!
Do you get tired of lies? Do you recognize how many lies you are

constantly being told? We have become desensitized to lying since it has become such a normal part of living. Lying is the outcome of people being right in their own eyes and stubbornly holding to their own viewpoint, **regardless of evidence to the contrary**.

Lies are constantly in politics and government, and we tend to simply accept it. Rarely does anyone address issues truthfully. And when such a rare thing does occur, **many simply do not want to hear the truth**. Politics and lying are quite synonymous. We are constantly being bombarded by little lies, big lies and every kind of shading of the truth that falls in between.

In talk shows, books, advertising, and the news—what is the truth?

How often do you find genuine truth, fidelity, honesty, and faithfulness in marital relationships? Again, how many lies? Over half of all marriages in the United States end in divorce. Are lies involved in such cases? Constantly!

Are there lies in the work place, in corporations and between employers and employees? People live with lies and deceit every day, and this very thing contributes mightily to the daily stress of life. Lies hurt relationships and cause people to be agitated and angry at one another.

How much stress is added to other areas of your life because of lies? What about relationships in families and the home, with children and parents, and between neighbors, friends or relatives?

The list is endless, but we simply don't stop to consider how such a thing impacts everyday life. The consequences are enormous and far greater than anyone can imagine.

So how long has it been since you were lied to by someone? How many minutes has it been?

Religion Is the Worst Offender
Religion is the greatest culprit of all when it comes to lying and deceit. You need to know why! It is for this very reason that this

earth is about to suffer more than it has at any other time in history.

Religion has had a devastating impact on people in all nations of the world. The clash of lying religions is about to erupt on a worldwide scale that will affect every person on earth. Why is this, and how is such a thing possible?

This book addresses religion because, whether you know it or not, *at this very time,* religion is at the heart and core of your life, even if you are not *religious.* Most people don't like to discuss this subject, much less mention the word "God." This book is not *religiously syrupy* or *preachy,* but it does candidly discuss religion and God; yet not in the manner you are accustomed to hearing. The truth is, religion **is** the greatest cause of suffering and evil in this world, and it is due to this that the greatest clash of religion the world has ever known is about to erupt.

Lies are going to be exposed by this book, and generally, when lies are exposed, people get mad. If some of these lies affect your life, which they will, what will you do? Will you get mad and upset, or will you honestly address those lies with the truth? Such moments in life are quite revealing. Can you objectively deal with the truth when you hear it? The truth is, most cannot!

Candidly, how you respond has much to do with what you will experience in the months and very few remaining years that follow. This is a time for man's judgment. It is not to be taken lightly.

One More Consideration

Before we continue, one additional matter needs to be made clear. Although I, the author, live in the United States, this book is not written with the prejudices or biases of an American. No national prejudice is affecting what is written here, nor any prejudice from any religion of this world.

This is important to understand since this book will be widely distributed and people around the world tend to be very distrusting of anything written by an American. People are just as distrusting in matters of religion, especially if the view is different from what they have always believed. All these feelings are normal and very understandable, but what you need to keep in mind are the things you read in the first chapter. This book does not originate from the prejudices of man; its message comes from the inspiration and revelation of God Almighty given to one of His prophets.

Why So Much Confusion?

Deception is at the very heart of the problems that exist among nations and religions of this world. Where, if any, is the truth and where are the lies?

No matter where people live on this earth, they have been lied to all their lives. This is true, whether it is on the job, in politics and government, or in families and communities; but it is most true in religion.

When it comes to religion, who is right; or is anyone right? When it comes to this subject, isn't it true that everyone believes he or she is right? And if someone is right, then others who believe differently are wrong.

Truth is at the very heart of this subject. By its very definition, only one thing can be true when it comes to God and His way. There cannot be many differing ideas about God and His word with all of them being right. Only one can be right! Only one can be true!

God told man that there is only one faith, one belief, one hope, one "good news" from God, and one God. If this is true, then there are big problems with this world's religions. God states what should be obvious, *"...no lie is of the truth"* (1 John 2:21).

To make this matter clear, if two religious organizations both claim to be Christian, but they are in opposition over any single doctrine, then by definition only one can possibly be true. This is important to understand so that you can see the magnitude of the problem in the examples given in this chapter.

A person's prejudice, concerning one's religious beliefs, will mostly depend upon where they were born in the world and the faith they were taught by their parents.

When I was about six years old, I remember reasoning: if there is no Easter Bunny, then Santa Claus must not be real either. If any parent teaches such things to their children, then at some early point in their lives they will learn that Santa Claus is not real—that he is a hoax. Is it any wonder I learned of more lies in traditional Christianity as I matured? If children are taught lies, then is it any wonder they learn to be skeptical and mistrusting?

Is there a God? Most would answer "yes." Then, if so, who is He and who is telling the truth about Him? Everyone should ask, "Does He have a spokesman on earth—someone He speaks through as He did in days of old?"

Do Catholics, who make up 1.2 billion people on earth, represent the true God? Is the Pope the true spokesman for God on earth? Or do the 1.3 billion believers of Islam have the true knowledge of the one God they call Allah? What about the remaining 1 billion people (separate from the number of those in the Catholic faith) who make up "traditional Christianity"? And what about the faith of 900 million in Hinduism, or the 400 million in China's traditional religion, or the 375 million in Buddhism, or the 14 million that comprise Judaism?

If we understand the definition of "truth," then we know we have a big problem in answering the question about one true belief. It should be abundantly clear that there are millions on earth who are deceived.

If there are thousands of separate organizations within "traditional Christianity" that differ greatly in doctrinal belief (and there are), then only one, if any, can possibly be true.

Are all these religious groups throughout the world worshipping the same God? NO! Their very beliefs and doctrines represent different teachings about God. All of them cannot be true. If they were all true, then they would be in agreement with one another.

Having one's origin in the God of Abraham does not make one true. There are over 3.5 billion people who claim such origin. Those who speak about the one and selfsame God do not teach the same things about Him. That is the problem! The reality is that there are billions on the earth who speak of God but do not teach the truth about Him, especially about what He says. Simply using the name of God or Jesus Christ does not make one true. Many use the name of the Creator God and His Son Jesus Christ, but they teach a false God and a false Christ.

Isn't it confusing? Is it any wonder that the world is in such chaos? Religious belief or no religious belief (which accounts for 1.1 billion people), it is *religious belief* that is at the very heart and core of this world's problems, whether you see it or not—believe it or not.

Let's consider what religious confusion and disagreement produces.

How well do Catholics and Protestants get along in Ireland? Do they believe in the same God or follow the same God?

Does the Church of England or the Catholic Church recognize the same government of God?

Is Shia or Sunni correct in their representation of Allah? Or do those who follow the ideals of al-Qaeda have Allah on their side? Who is right? Who is true?

Do Mormons believe in the same God as the Baptists or the Seventh Day Adventists?

Do Reformed Jews agree with the Orthodox, or vise-versa?

All of these believe they are true and right before God, yet their doctrines and basic beliefs are often vastly different. They do not teach about the same God because each teaches that God has taught it "truth" which is different from all others. If that were not true and they did believe the same, then wouldn't they be able to join together in the same faith (belief)?

During World War II, how is it that priests of the Catholic Church blessed German and Italian soldiers who were going into war to kill Americans, who had themselves been blessed by their priests in the Catholic Church? How can such a thing be? Is there hypocrisy in such things? Does such a thing reflect a unified teaching, from one God, with those of the same faith? Obviously, this example does not fit the definition of a unified belief in one true doctrine from one true God. So what is the truth?

Do you see the dilemma? Do you see why there is so much confusion? Can you begin to see how this affects your life?

Patrick Cockburn's article, "Iraq's top Shia cleric warns of 'genocidal war,'" was reported in the *Independent News* (19 July 2005) and reveals the religious confusion surrounding the ongoing terrorism in Iraq:

> The slaughter of hundreds of civilians by suicide bombers shows that a "genocidal war" is threatening Iraq, Grand Ayatollah Ali al-Sistani, the country's most influential Shia cleric, warned yesterday.

> So far he has persuaded most of his followers not to respond in kind against the Sunni, from whom the bombers are drawn, despite repeated massacres of Shia. But sectarian divisions between Shia and Sunni are deepening across Iraq after the killing of 18 children in the district of New Baghdad last week and the death of 98 people caught by the explosion of a gas tanker in the market town of Musayyib. Many who died were visiting a Shia mosque.

> Against the wishes of the Grand Ayatollah, who has counselled restraint, some Shia have started retaliatory killings of members of the former regime, most of whom but not all are Sunni. Some carrying out the attacks

appear to belong to the 12,000-strong paramilitary police commandos.

This news article is certainly reflective of the confusion that exists in religion. Religious differences are at the core of festering distrust and hatreds that will soon erupt into world war. More will be given on this in another chapter.

In 2002, an ongoing conflict of religious ideologies led up to the brink of all out war between the nuclear powers of India and Pakistan. The conflict between Muslim and Hindu has manifested itself because of deeply-held religious beliefs over the region of Kashmir.

In this one area of the world alone, peace is fragile. Much of the world has been deeply concerned at what could happen if Pakistan were to lose President Musharraf as leader through an assassination attempt, and such attempts have already occurred. This is a nation in deep religious conflict with non-Muslim minorities and vastly differing Islamic ideologies.

What about Iran and its growing nuclear hunger? Does religion influence this thirst for greater power that could ultimately be wielded in this world? And what will Israel's response be? One should not have to ask the question, "Does religion play a part in all this?"

What about the ever-present stress between Israel and the Muslim world that surrounds her? Jerusalem is far from being the city of peace that her name means.

The world has always been filled with religious dilemma. Confusion has reigned in the hearts of men. Is there really a God of the earth? If so, which one is He? Who is right? Why is there such diversity and vastly opposing views of God among religious beliefs? Is God so small and so weak that He cannot make the truth known? **You need to answer such questions!**

Confusion In Religion

It may not be easy for you to continue reading. You may recognize and readily agree to the confusion and deception that you see in the religious beliefs of others. But when it comes to what you believe, can you admit error when it is pointed out to you? Most people cannot, because interference with one's **personal** religious beliefs is more than they can bear.

Most people simply cannot admit error in personally-held religious beliefs. When people are in error, their deeply-held prejudices make it nearly impossible for them to acknowledge that they have embraced lies from very early in life.

We are now going to delve more deeply into the "sacred" realm of personally-held religious beliefs. Questioning one's religious beliefs is highly offensive to most people.

It was stated earlier that this book was not being written from any influence from any of the religions of this world. However, it is written from revelation from the one and only true God of all eternity. People in this world do not know their roots, true identity or the true history of their existence.

To Islam, Allah is God and this God is one. Allah is the Arabic word for God and simply means the supreme and only God, the creator, who according to the Qur'an is the same as the God of the Bible—the God of Abraham.

Those of Judaism believe that God is one, but call Him by the Hebrew words of El and Yahweh.

Both Islam and Judaism share the truth that the one true God is the God of Abraham, but other understanding has become deeply clouded over the centuries.

Different languages do not alter the truth. If anyone refers to the one true God of eternity, who was the Allah of Abraham or the El of Abraham, then they are referring to the same one true God—the Creator of all the universe.

Both peoples have their roots in the God of Abraham, who is the one and only true eternal God. There is no other eternal living

God. So why are their beliefs so different when both recognize they have sprung from Abraham and proclaim they follow the same God of Abraham?

Why such confusion and bitterness toward one another? This is a centuries-old story.

Abraham and Sarah were promised a son through whom God would work, but as Abraham (Abram) grew old and Sarah was beyond age to conceive, the time seemed to have passed them by for any possibility to have a son. So they agreed that Sarah's handmaid, Hagar, an Egyptian, could give Abraham a son. The story is found in Genesis 16 in the Bible.

Sarah actually gave her handmaid to Abraham to be his wife, but when Hagar conceived, her attitude changed and she began to despise Sarah. With Abraham's permission, Sarah confronted her handmaid; and as a result of this harsh confrontation, Hagar fled into the wilderness.

You need to know what happened next because the events that followed laid the groundwork for two great religions in the world. These two religions carried deeply-held bitterness and envying with them from that time forward, and it has existed through the ages.

A messenger of God came to Hagar by a fountain of water in the wilderness of Shur and asked, "From where do you come and where will you now go?" She explained that she had fled from her mistress, Sarah, but the messenger of God replied to her, "Return to your mistress and submit yourself unto her hands." The messenger then continued with God's instruction for her, "I will multiply your seed exceedingly, that it shall not be able to be numbered because of such multitude of people." The messenger added, "Behold you are with child, and you shall bear a son, and you shall call his name Ishmael [meaning, "God shall hear"] because the Eternal One has heard your affliction."

Although Hagar went back to Sarah as the messenger said, the rift between the two women continued; and since then, the same spirit has been passed along. It is one of envy, distrust, competition, pride, jealousy, and bitterness. This spirit has literally been passed on from generation to generation through both peoples.

Islam sprang out of Abraham through Hagar. Since God's word is true, the descendants of Hagar, through Ishmael, have become great on the earth. It is impossible to make an exact count of every descendent because they cover such a vast region throughout the Middle East and other areas of the world. Today, these same descendants have grown into greater power and influence because of the abundance of oil they have been blessed to possess. Due to oil, the world has given them more recognition. It is a shame that such a thing has to happen before others finally begin to show the consideration and respect they should have shown all along. Man can truly be cruel to man.

These descendents of Abraham, through Hagar, know that the audience they have received from the western world is not very genuine, but only the result of the world's reliance on oil. Mankind is a very selfish creature!

These attitudes in the world are the reason why much of the world of Islam has turned to deep resentment and bitterness, especially toward the western world. It is easy to understand, if you're willing to admit it; but on the other hand, it does not justify jihad against others. Yes, there is deep-rooted bitterness, and understandably so; but if people want to truly make peace, then they must learn to submit to the will of God. God's will for man is that he turn to a genuine spirit of humility and a true willingness to *work* at making peace. Peace does not come naturally. The God of Abraham plainly declares that man does not know the way of peace.

Many teachings in the world have their roots in the Word of God. Islam means "submission to the will of God." Those who truly follow the path of submission will be blessed. What was stated by their own Prophet Mohammed is true, "The best jihad is the one who struggles against his own self for Allah." He understood that the noblest battle anyone could ever hope to enter into is that of fighting against **one's** own "selfish" human nature in order to yield oneself to God—in obedience to God.

Muslims greet each other with "slam alaikum," which means "peace be with you." Although such a greeting is good, peace does not come by well wishing, but by visible actions that help make it a reality. It is true that peace between the descended half-brothers of the two sons of Abraham will not be brought about by man's efforts, but first by God's intervention to humble both so that they will work toward peace—God's way and with His help. This centuries-old rift cannot be healed by man's own efforts, even if man genuinely tried to do so.

The One who is recognized in the beginning of the Qur'an as "Master of the Day of Judgment" is about to pass out judgment upon mankind by overthrowing every government of man. It is also a true saying that, *"if anyone harms (others), God will harm him, and if anyone shows hostility to others, God will show hostility to him"* (Sunan of Abu-Dawood, Hadith 1625). Be careful how you follow God in the few remaining years before God overthrows man's world.

There are teachings in Islam, Judaism and Christianity that clearly have their roots in the truth that originates from the God of Abraham; but as we continue, it will become abundantly clear that these major religions have strayed very far from the God of Abraham.

The Other Half-Brother

Abraham was 86 years old when Ishmael was born. When he was 99 God told him about a son He would give him through Sarah, through whom many nations would spring. Only one of those nations would become Judah—the modern-day Jewish people. The other people and nations will be explained later.

When Abraham was told that Sarah would indeed bear him a son, he asked God to please consider working only through Ishmael so that Sarah would not have to go through the ordeal of bearing a child in her old age. But God told Abraham that Ishmael would indeed be blessed and He would multiply him mightily by making him a great nation. It would be a nation of people that would spring out of 12 princes, who themselves would grow into distinct nations, making up a great nation of (primarily) Arabic peoples.

But it was also the One Eternal God's purpose to raise up an additional 12 nations that would, in time, spring out of Abraham's son, whom he was to call Isaac.

As soon as Isaac was weaned, Sarah became jealous of Ishmael and pushed Abraham into banishing Hagar and Ishmael. This grieved Abraham deeply, but God told him to go ahead and do it. From that time forward, neither lineage dealt with each other with genuine care and concern; instead, animosity and deep-rooted attitudes were passed down, through both, from generation to generation. This result is because mankind has not understood the true will of God and His purpose being worked out on this earth. All have failed to follow the way of peace which comes from God. Mankind does not grasp God's purpose that He is working out through those 24 nations that have sprung out of Abraham.

Although Judaism is one of the smaller religions on the earth with about 14,000,000 followers, it stirs up more controversy and disdain than any other religion. This small group, that follows Judaism, sprang from only one of the 12 nations that came out of Abraham, through Isaac, and then his son, Jacob.

It will be covered later, but the other 11 nations that sprang out of Abraham, through Jacob, have always polluted the ways of God and removed Him far from their own selfish pursuits. However, the nation of Judah has been quite outspoken in their adherence to the one true God of Abraham. Although they have been far ahead of their eleven brothers, holding to a belief in the

God of Abraham, they have drifted far from the true will of God—and the truth.

The Jewish people use the first five books of the Bible more than what is covered in the Psalms and Prophets. If the Jewish people are honest with their beliefs, then they must acknowledge that they are not obedient to the law in some of the most basic doctrine.

In reality, the book of Leviticus has little meaning for Judaism, yet it is the third book of the law. Have their teachers and Rabbis tried to follow the law of offerings and sacrifices? What are the excuses for not doing so if they truly believe in the law that they vigorously profess? There is a lineage of Levites among the Jewish people, but where is the priesthood? And how can the law be followed without a high priest? Where is the unity of belief? Where are the priests? Is this way of life null and void because there is no temple? Is their obedience to the physical performance of the law of sacrifices without meaning, since they do not practice it? Does prayer, as some suggest, replace obedience to the book of Leviticus? Where is that stated in God's law?

If there is presently no temple where they can serve God, can they not serve God in a temporary one, as in the wilderness? The true answers to these questions reveal the magnitude of the problem. It is their paradox because by the law they know they have no authority to build a temple—not even a temporary one. If God has not made such a thing possible for Judaism—if God has not given them a temple, then has God abandoned them? Is God unable to deliver those whom He will, especially if they are His own people who are following Him in truth? And if He will not, what is the answer?

Of all people, the Jewish people have been promised much by God because it is promised that through Abraham, and then through the lineage of David (who was of the nation of Judah), that the Messiah would come. This promise is on a spiritual plane, which is far above the promises given to Judah's brother, Joseph, which are of a national nature, and on a physical plane. But the understanding of this spiritual promise has been clouded by time and false teaching. What is the truth? It has been lost by Judaism for one main reason! It is due to this spiritual promise, and Judah's rejection of it, that the God of Abraham is about to come and overthrow the government of Israel (of the literal nation Israel), which is today controlled by the one ancient nation of Judah—the Jews.

What a paradox! If you are practicing any form of Judaism, you need to humbly consider what is being said here because, of all people, you have no excuse. You have been lied to by your teachers for several hundred years now. Don't you have just a little curiosity about what these lies are? And don't presume you already know the complete answer.

The False Teaching
For Judaism, the real basis of the problem and great false teaching is this: Judaism claims to truly follow the God of Abraham, but doesn't observe Passover as God instructed in Leviticus 23, *"In the fourteenth day of the first month at even* (Heb. "between the evenings"–ben ha arbayim) *is the Lord's Passover"* (Lev. 23:4). Instead, Judaism observes Passover after the fourteenth day, on the beginning of the fifteenth, which is the first day of Unleavened Bread—a High Day—an annual Sabbath. But God clearly says it is to be observed **in** the fourteenth day.

If you keep Passover, when do you begin its observance? Does it begin before or after sunset of the 14th day of the first month? If you are one of those who starts this observance before sundown on the 14th, how much of your service is actually **in** the 14th and how much is **in** the 15th?

Of all people, those of Judaism, who keep the weekly seventh-day Sabbath, know when the Sabbath begins and when it ends.

They don't need a Rabbi to tell them what this command means because they have grown up with the knowledge of sunset to sunset in the counting of this Holy Day. There is one exception to this; some Rabbis teach a six p.m. to six p.m. observance for the Sabbath, regardless of when the sun sets, but even a child would understand that such reasoning is not obedience to God's instruction.

Any correctly kept Sabbath observance among those in Judaism is between the two evenings. The beginning of "even" is when the sun sets on the sixth day. The Sabbath begins at the very time of sunset and lasts until the following "even," which ends the seventh day. This is their own definition of "ben ha erbayim." However, they will not acknowledge it for the observance of Passover, but they do acknowledge it for the weekly Sabbath and annual Holy Days.

Passover is recognized as one of the holiest days in Judaism, but it is observed on the wrong day and not even in the way they are instructed. Those who follow Judaism have followed the false doctrines of their teachers. Most of them don't even know their history of how this change came about, moving the observance of Passover from the beginning of the evening on the fourteenth to the immediate period following the fourteenth, in the beginning of the evening on the fifteenth.

None of this is said as an attack on Jewish people, but it is said out of love that they might acknowledge their wrong ways, repent and truly turn to the one true God of all the earth—the true God of Abraham. Judaism has lost sight of God's true will and His spiritual promises because of their disobedience to God's instruction concerning the Passover observance.

Does Christianity Hold the Key?

Christianity comprises 2.2 billion people on earth, yet they do not agree among themselves about God or Jesus Christ because their beliefs (faith) vary with thousands of opposing doctrines. Is one of them true? If they disagree with one another in doctrine about what is the true word of God, then by the very definition of "truth" they cannot all be true. If the world is not already in enough chaos and confusion when it comes to religion, then certainly Christianity has made it many, many times worse!

Christian "faith" is about what one "believes" concerning Christianity. If people *believe* they are to worship God in a church on Sunday, then that is their *faith*—they will live by that *belief* and attend worship services on Sunday.

If a Christian believes that the Bible, and primarily the New Testament, is the inspired word of God and that they are to live by every word of God (as the scripture says), then they would want to obey what God instructs. If there is one true religion and it is one of the Christian faiths, which one is it? Surely, it would be the one that follows God's word "faithfully" as it is given in scripture.

The examples one can use to address this question are endless; most certainly they cannot all be covered in a book this size. Instead, it would take volumes! But let's look at some examples and see if we can find a "true" Church that is the "true" religion on earth. Let's look at several examples so that we can begin to grasp the scope of the real problem.

The Catholic faith comprises a little over one-half (1.2 billion) of all that is called Christianity. Therefore, it is of primary importance that we consider this faith when we speak of Christianity. This will prove to be of great importance as we proceed through this area of comparison.

The Catholic doctrine of purgatory is a belief (faith) that some die with smaller faults, for which there has been no repentance, and upon death go to a place of purgatory rather than directly to heaven or hell. The Catholic Encyclopedia states that the church "has from the Sacred Scriptures...that there is a purgatory."

However, the Methodist plainly state in their articles of belief that there is no scriptural evidence of purgatory:

The Romish [speaking of the Catholic Church] doctrine concerning purgatory, pardon, worshiping, and adoration, as well of images as of relics, and also invocation of saints, is a fond thing, vainly invented, and grounded upon no warrant of Scripture, but repugnant to the Word of God. (Article XIV.—Of Purgatory)

The Methodist clearly teach that the doctrine of purgatory is "vainly invented" and "repugnant to the Word of God." Most Protestant churches agree with this same stance of the Methodist faith.

Obviously, these two faiths (beliefs) are diametrically opposite to each other. To be the true followers of God and "faithful" to His word, only one of these can possibly be true. Either one is true, or both are false; but both cannot be true.

It is important that everyone consider some of the most basic doctrinal differences in a faith that calls itself "Christian." Each faith (group) believes it is right, yet these faiths (groups) differ greatly from each other. Therefore, only one can possibly be considered true. Stated another way, either one is true and the others are false, or all must be false.

The Catholic faith is one of the oldest known "Christian" faiths. None of the Protestant churches have the long history of the Catholic Church. The Lutheran Church, which is the oldest Protestant church, broke away from the Catholic Church. Many others eventually broke from the Catholic faith because they embraced a different faith—one never known before. The faith of the Lutheran Church didn't exist until Martin Luther came on the scene and stated his "faith" about God. Today, we find that most "Christian" faiths came directly from the Catholic Church or from splinter groups of other "Christian" faiths during the last two centuries.

All the "Christian" churches that embrace Sunday worship, Easter and Christmas observance, and the Trinity doctrine received these doctrines through the Catholic Church; yet all these churches believe that many doctrines, which the Catholic Church embraces to be spiritually true, are false.

Let's notice other great conflicts that exist among the various religious groups which believe they are the true representatives of Christianity.

The Sabbath Question

The Seventh Day Adventist Church has some conflicting practices among themselves, but the one they have built their name upon regards the timing of their weekly Sabbath observance. This is a matter of strong belief (faith) on their part.

Although most Seventh Day Adventists in the United States believe it is permissible to observe the annual period of Christmas and Easter, many of their brethren in other countries vehemently disagree. But they do all agree that the seventh-day Sabbath observance reflects whether one is in the true Church or not. Notice some of the strong language they use when speaking of the seventh-day Sabbath opposed to the observance of Sunday worship:

> The change of the Sabbath is the sign or mark of the authority of the Romish church [Catholic Church] . . . The keeping of the counterfeit Sabbath is the reception of the mark. (Ellen G. White, *Great Controversy*, Vol. 4: 281)

> Sunday-keeping must be the mark of the beast . . . The reception of his mark must be something that involves the greatest offense that can be committed against God. (Elder U. Smith, *The Marvel of Nations*: 170, 183)

The Sunday Sabbath is purely a child of the Papacy. It is the mark of the beast. (*Advent Review*, Vol. I, No. 2, August, 1850)

Sunday-keeping is an institution of the first beast, and ALL who submit to obey this institution emphatically worship the first beast and receive his mark, "the mark of the beast." . . . Those who worship the beast and his image by observing the first day are certainly idolaters, as were the worshippers of the golden calf. (*Advent Review Extra*, August, 1850: 10-11)

Here we find the mark of the beast. The very act of changing the Sabbath into Sunday, on the part of the Catholic Church, without any authority from the Bible. (Ellen G. White, *The Mark of the Beast*: 23)

Are you beginning to get a much deeper sense of the enormous confusion that exists, not only in the religions of this world, but especially the faith that calls itself "Christian?" If you were to look at the hundreds, and even thousands, of varying and opposing Christian beliefs (faiths), you would indeed see that all of them disagree with each other. There is no other conclusion; all of them cannot be true. If one is true, then indeed, all the others are false and full of lies.

As previously stated about the Seventh Day Adventists, they have a common belief in the seventh day as their weekly Sabbath; but in some areas of the world, they disagree about the observance of Christmas and Easter.

It is true that there is no mention of either of these observances in the Bible. It is also true that both of them have come from the Catholic Church, and that neither one comes from any authority stated in scripture. Even the name "Christmas" shows its origin, which comes from the "Mass of Christ."

So if you are one of the thousands among the Christian faiths, do you have "faith" in the observance of Easter and Christmas, or mass for that matter? If you do believe, does it matter to you that the authority for the observance of Christmas and Easter comes from the Pope and the Catholic Church?

If you do not believe in the authority of the Catholic Church to establish doctrines for the faith of your church, then why do you believe so many of the doctrines this early church established? If you do believe the Catholic Church has authority from God to establish many of the doctrines of most other "Christian" churches, then why don't you fully submit to her complete authority and leave the false one that you have been embracing?

It really adds up to confusion, doesn't it? But the bottom line is that you, and you alone, are accountable for what you believe. Only you can decide for yourself what is true and what is false. To do so, you must be truthful with yourself about your long-held religious beliefs; and most of all, you must be truthful to God because, as your Bible says, *"...no lie is of the truth"* (1 John 2:21). This should be obvious if a person genuinely seeks to be truthful. If some doctrine or belief in God is a lie, then by its very definition it cannot be true or from God.

The Faith of the Trinity
People who embrace any of the thousands of "Christian" beliefs need to know what their church teaches, where their beliefs originate, and whether they truly come from God. If they find lies, then they must change or willingly submit to what they know is false, and thereby be guilty of opposing the one true God.

The scriptures upon which most "Christians" base their faith says, *"God is a Spirit: and they that worship Him must worship Him in spirit and in truth"* (John 4:24). If someone knowingly holds to a false teaching, then they certainly cannot be worshiping God "in truth." God does not accept such worship!

You need to understand that the doctrine of the Trinity does not have its origin in any of the Protestant churches, but solely in the Catholic Church. Therefore, most of traditional Christianity has accepted this doctrine as truth from the Catholic Church.

The *Catholic Encyclopedia* under "The Blessed Trinity" states:

> The Trinity is the term employed to signify the central doctrine of the Christian religion—the truth that in the unity of the Godhead there are Three Persons, the Father, the Son, and the Holy Spirit, these Three Persons being truly distinct one from another.

Again, the origin of this *central doctrine* is in the Catholic Church. All other Christian organizations that believe the doctrine of the Trinity received it solely from the Catholic Church, which began to embrace it in the third and fourth centuries A.D.

This same article, "The Blessed Trinity," also says, "In Scripture there is as yet no single term by which the Three Divine Persons are denoted together." The article is explaining that there is no such term as "trinity" in scripture and that there is no such depiction of the Father, Son, and Holy Spirit in such terms.

The same article in the *Catholic Encyclopedia* adds:

> The Vatican Council further defined that the Christian Faith contains mysteries strictly so called (can. 4). All theologians admit that the doctrine of the Trinity is of the number of these. Indeed, of all revealed truths this is the most impenetrable to reason. Hence, to declare this to be no mystery would be a virtual denial of the canon in question.

Although such articles of the Catholic Church are not plainly written, they are clearly stating that the doctrine of the Trinity is a mystery which cannot be readily discerned by human reasoning.

They see this doctrine as being so obscure in scripture that it must instead be divinely revealed.

That is why this same article on the Trinity continues by its discussion of the term *mystery*, and states:

> The Vatican Council has explained the meaning to be attributed to the term *mystery* in theology. It lays down that a mystery is a truth which we are not merely incapable of discovering apart from Divine Revelation, but which, even when revealed, remains "hidden by the veil of faith and enveloped, so to speak, by a kind of darkness" (Const., "De fide. cath.", iv).

Thus, the Catholic Church clearly states that the Trinity is not a Biblical term, but only a revealed doctrine. The Catholic faith is that the Trinity was revealed through the office of the Pope to their Church. Why do so many in traditional Christianity accept this from the Catholic Church, along with many other non-Biblical doctrines, but will not accept her authority over them?

Some traditional Christian organizations oppose the Trinity doctrine. The Jehovah Witnesses are one of these. In *Watch Tower*, a Jehovah Witness publication, an article entitled, "Should You Believe in the Trinity?", reveals that they clearly reject the authority of the Catholic Church and the Trinity doctrine:

> After some discussion the question was asked, "If the Trinity is not a Biblical teaching, how did it become a doctrine of Christendom?"

> He [Emperor Theodosius] established the creed of the Council of Nicaea as the standard for his realm and

convened the Council of Constantinople in 381 C.E. to clarify the formula [for the Trinity doctrine].

That council agreed to place the holy spirit on the same level as God and Christ. For the first time, Christendom's Trinity began to come into focus.

WHY, for thousands of years, did none of God's prophets teach his people about the Trinity? At the latest, would Jesus not use his ability as the Great Teacher to make the Trinity clear to his followers? Would God inspire hundreds of pages of Scripture and yet not use any of this instruction to teach the Trinity if it were the "central doctrine" of faith?

Are Christians to believe that centuries after Christ and after having inspired the writing of the Bible, God would back the formulation of a doctrine that was unknown to his servants for thousands of years, one that is an "inscrutable mystery" "beyond the grasp of human reason," one that admittedly had a pagan background and was "largely a matter of church politics"?

The testimony of history is clear: The Trinity teaching is a deviation from the truth, an apostatizing from it. (www.watchtower.org/library/ti/article_04.htm)

Clearly, the Jehovah Witnesses do not accept the doctrine of a Trinity that originated in the Catholic Church, yet they do accept the Catholic doctrine of Sunday as their day of worship. Those in Christianity who uphold Sunday observance received this belief through the Catholic Church, which began several hundred years before any of them were established. The Catholics clearly state, in their own encyclopedia, that the Bible gives no scriptural authority for changing the observance of the seventh-day Sabbath to an observance on the first day of the week (Sunday). They candidly acknowledge that this change was made through the authority of the Catholic Church.

Why do many in Christianity stubbornly hold to the Catholic observance of Sunday? Why do they feel they must defend this doctrine themselves by twisting and misrepresenting scriptures so that they seemingly indicate that there is some validity in a Sunday observance? The fact is: the Catholic Church is correct when they say there is no scriptural evidence for such a change. Nowhere does scripture give a commandment to observe Sunday as the day of worship, instead of the Sabbath. Ask any preacher what scriptural authority gives anyone that right, and you will have encountered an uncomfortable, unhappy preacher.

Doctrinal confusion continues as you investigate what various organizations teach as the Word of God. The Almighty God states that He is not the author of confusion (1 Corinthians 14:33), yet this world is deeply confused concerning His word, His truth and His way of life.

The more you learn about the differences in doctrines within Christianity, as well as their origins, the more lies and deception you will discover. Do yourself a favor and check an encyclopedia for words like Christmas, Easter, Trinity, and Sabbath and see what you learn. You will find that some doctrines of traditional Christianity have much of their origin in paganism. These things don't seem to bother people, but it should! If something is not *fully* of God, then it is not of God, and it is not true!

The Truth!
The truth is: people don't like the truth. This has been man's way for nearly 6,000 years. That is the true witness of the nature of man. This is the true testimony of God from the creation of man, until now. And now, that judgment is coming on mankind because of this very thing. You just happen to live at the very

time that this judgment is going to be administered and in a powerful way. God has a plan and a purpose in letting man go so long in his own resistance to His will and His way of life. Now is the time for all of this to be corrected.

So what is the truth? This book is the truth! It is one of the primary things I do appreciate about the job God has given me. I am simply to state the truth **as it is**. I do not have to spend endless hours defending it, debating it or expounding upon it. The truth is simply the truth, and now, you can begin to see it more clearly and respond if you have any desire or hope to receive favor from God in the time of destruction that is almost upon us.

Yes, this book is the truth. God is about to prove that this book is telling the truth! He will do so with power unleashed beyond any that He has ever used to reveal to man that He is their Creator.

Nearly everyone reading this book will not be able to escape the reality that you are wrong in much of what you believe concerning God. This will not be easy for you to admit as God corrects you. How much suffering will you have to go through before you will begin to acknowledge what is true? How much suffering will you experience before you drop to your knees in repentance before God to acknowledge your pride, stubbornness and refusal to obey what is true—that which is from Him?

Remember, God is merciful to those who are broken in spirit (broken from a spirit of pride), humble and teachable before Him, and who seek to obey Him in the truth. If you are not willing to humble yourself, He will humble you. You are not greater than God. He is greater than you! If people put Him to the test, especially at this time in all human history, they will lose. This is true because the time of man's judgment is at hand at the end of 6,000 years of self-rule. Now is the time God has chosen to begin revealing Himself fully to this world.

The history of man is: he does not believe what God has said. God gave 6,000 years to man to live his own way. Now, all of that is about to change. The true witness of all man's history is that man has not listened or wanted God to rule in his life.

The witness now is: God will bring an end to man's rule and establish His own rule over all the earth. That is God's judgment upon man. Now is the time for God's rule to begin as God reveals to man that what He has told man for 6,000 years is indeed true!

God has extended His patience to man and his ways, however, God has a set time for His plan which is coming to an end—and very soon! The time of God's judgment upon man's disobedience is now going to be administered with power like the earth has never witnessed. As bad as it will be for the world during the great tribulation that is coming, we can look forward to the joy and fullness of a beautiful world just beyond it. Hopefully, you will have the opportunity to be part of that new world.

Chapter 3

TIME HAS RUN OUT FOR MAN

The true history of man is not what you have been taught at school. What have you been taught concerning your history?

Much of what we learn about the history of man depends upon where we live. If you live in China, the history taught is much different from the history taught in Japan, whether it is recent or ancient. What someone is taught in Israel is different from what one is taught in Germany or Egypt. The history of man is different in Greece than it is in Italy. And so it goes.

Man manipulates his outlook on the past by his vision of the present and the future. As shown in the last chapter, there are many lies about our history—the history of man.

As an aside, yet pertinent to the subject of this chapter and something that will be covered more thoroughly later, it is due to the European viewpoint of European history, that a new Europe is arising. Other areas of the world are ignorant of the growing forces in the heart of Europe that are working for a "United States of Europe." This is important to understand because it has much to do with a rapidly approaching World War III.

The heart of Europe thirsts for a revived Europe of old, and God has revealed that they will attain it and become the strongest power the earth has even known. Even as I write, only yesterday there was news from Europe that reported on a Belgian leader's new book. "In a bid to go against the eurosceptic tide that is dominating EU public opinion, Belgian prime minister Guy Verhofstadt has pleaded for the creation of a federal 'United States of Europe.' Mr. Verhofstadt, a liberal, on Thursday (December 1, 2005) presented his new book, provocatively entitled 'The United States of Europe.'"

This leader, and many others like him, embrace a billowing passion for a powerful United Europe. This insatiable thirst is fueled, in large part, by deep roots from their past, which inflame a burning desire for a renewed future.

History is unique in the eyes of the beholder, but man's true history can only be seen through the truth of his relationship with God. This is the reason man is blind to his true history; he has not wanted God to have too close of a relationship with him. Through time, many have used the name of God, but have not wanted to do as He said. The hypocrisy in man runs very deep.

Man's True History

The reality is that you can only understand what is true in man's history when you know how God has been working with man through the ages. Through time, man has not acknowledged his own beginning! He chooses to ignore it. Far too many people say they believe in God, yet they choose to believe they crawled out of slime and evolved into man. Not only has man not accepted the truth about his own beginning, he has not accepted the truth about each step along the way.

God said concerning man, *"And even as they did not like to retain God in their knowledge, God gave them over to a reprobate mind"* (Roman 1:28). In these verses, God is simply saying that since man does not choose to know Him, then He (God) will release man (distance Himself from man) so that man can experience the consequences of his wrong choices, resulting in human suffering and the pollution of his mind.

As a result of man choosing to keep God completely out of the picture, or at least at a more comfortable distance away, he has twisted and misrepresented his history in order to insure that God is kept at bay. Rather than acknowledging that any of his existence is connected to God, man has fashioned history to reflect his own vanity and pride.

To make this point clear, you need to ask, "How many history books tell of man's true beginning?" How many teach about our first parents, Adam and Eve? Do you get the point? How sick is man when he will not even accept the beginning that God said He gave to man? Do you truly believe that man likes to retain the knowledge of God—his very Creator? This is precisely why man has now entered the final stage of his end-time judgment in 6,000 years of botched history!

So, how truthful is our history? Man doesn't accept the story of Adam and Eve as part of his history. He does not accept or teach the history of Noah and the flood. These two things alone keep man from learning the most basic lessons of life. History should teach us how to live in the present, as well as the future. As some people in the world have experienced, after it was too late, if we do not learn from the mistakes (lessons) of the past, we are destined to repeat them. This is exactly what has been going on ever since we were put on this earth—a complete failure to learn from our mistakes and turn to God.

As in the movie, *Groundhog Day*, man has been living life, repeating the past (our history) over, and over, and over, trying to get it right, except we never do. This is why God is now going to intervene and save us from ourselves.

God is going to bring an end to 6,000 years of man's way, man's government, man's religion, and man's own self-inflicted misery. You live at the pinnacle of all human history. Before man was ever created, God purposed to allow him to have his own governments and religions for a 6,000 year period. This time has come and is almost complete. **Time has run out for man!**

God has exercised great patience with man, *during this time*, in order to accomplish great things in His ultimate purpose for him. The first phase of this plan is to help us learn, from such a long history, that we are incapable of successfully governing ourselves. All of man's governments and religions have failed. God is giving us a great gift by letting us learn this lesson. For without learning this lesson, we cannot eventually go on to the much greater things He has in store for us. Only when that lesson is learned can we finally begin to attain lasting peace and true happiness.

Indeed, God has had great patience with mankind because the reality is: **we are not owed life.** It is not something we inherently deserve. **It is a gift from God**.

Since man has chosen to leave God out of his history, this book will fill in much of the gap so you can better grasp why we are in the end-time, what is coming next, and why.

God's Revelation and His Prophets

God told Noah to build an ark (a great ship). Noah was told to tell others that God had instructed him to build it, and that He (God) was going to bring a great flood upon the earth because of man's sinful ways. No one took what Noah said seriously, except his immediate family.

Moses was told to go to both the Israelites and the Egyptians and tell them that God had sent him to them. It took a while before they began to believe him.

God has sent His prophets to different people over and over again, and each time, God has told His prophets to make it very clear that what they (the prophets) were telling them (the people) was absolutely from God and to them.

After centuries of not hearing from one of God's prophets, the time has come once again—one last time—to hear the words of God and what He is about to do. It is the ultimate revelation of 6,000 years. This time of final revelation involves the accumulation of all the prophets of old, along with the majority of their prophecies that pertain to this time now. It is the most momentous time in all human history. It is the time when God will finally reveal Himself far more fully to man than He ever has before—many times more!

God's two end-time prophets will exercise great power, both in power displayed on the earth and in power of the revelation of God—more than all other prophets combined. This is how momentous these times are which we have now entered.

As I have stated, I am one of those prophets, and I am also the spokesman of both. That which I am telling you is not of me; **it is from the God of Abraham**—the Almighty God of the Universe.

My job is not to appease others. My job is not being done with pretentious piety as many religious leaders do. It is not being done in haughtiness or pride because this is not about vanity, ego, or illusions of grandeur. Simply said, this is not about me—it is about God—it is from God. Even this may be interpreted as haughty or egotistical to some, since everything is and will be accomplished through great boldness from God, and through great power given by Him to me.

You have before you a great opportunity. You can ponder the words spoken to you and let God show you they are true, or you can resist and experience the harsh consequences that all unrepentant and pride-filled humans will experience. Whether you receive these words or not, there will still be suffering. But it is wise, more than at any other time in all earth's history, to seek God with meekness and humility so that you might receive His favor and mercy. This time of judgment is not the time to resist God and oppose what He says and what He is doing. You will not win! All who refuse Him will be broken, even if it requires death.

God is merciful and filled with love toward all mankind in ways that you cannot even begin to imagine. But God cannot give His mercy and love to people until they acknowledge their wrong ways and begin to seek His.

Man has escaped God's direct correction for centuries because of His great patience in His overall plan for him. We are at the end of 6,000 years in that plan, and before the next great phase can be accomplished, all of man's governments and religions must be brought to an end. This is the time in which we now live. This is your reality!

God will prove whom He sends. Just as prophetic events will unfold with increasing power and frequency, so will I increase in power and recognition by others because of the job God has placed before me. It is God's purpose, and **He will do it**. Either I am an eloquent, rationally-sounding lunatic or I am sent from God. The clarity, orderliness and rationale of what you are reading is testimony in itself that this is from God. And if all of this is indeed from God, would it be wise to ignore it?

What's Next?

To understand what is coming next, you need to understand where we are now in prophecy. For this, you need to know about the Seals of Revelation.

The Book of Revelation was written by the Apostle John in the 90's A.D., after God had given him this revelation when he was exiled on the Isle of Patmos. John wrote about Seven Seals that would be opened at the end-time—at this time now!

The first five seals, as explained more fully in *The Prophesied End-Time,* concerned God's true Church. Those seals have already been opened. The message and revelation of those five seals was not for the world. It was exclusively for the Church. The world was unaware of what happened because it was and still is unaware of God's one and only true Church.

At this present time, six seals have been opened; but because the world is so far removed from God, it has not recognized the events that have been unfolding during this period of time. These very events are leading up to the opening of the Seventh Seal and the greatest time of destruction the world has ever known.

Even as God's own Church was caught completely off guard when the Seals of Revelation began to be opened, the world will be caught off guard when the Seventh Seal is opened.

At this very moment in writing, it has been precisely eleven years since the First Seal of Revelation was opened. It was opened on December 17, 1994. If you react to the recent history of God's Church and the opening of the first five seals without interest, then you will be deeply mistaken. You do need to know what has happened over the past eleven years because there is a similar "type" of prophetic destruction that is about to come upon the whole world.

The opening of the **First Seal** was the beginning of an apostasy (falling away from the truth) and great spiritual destruction upon God's Church. The opening of this seal served as a warning and an announcement **to God's people** that the end-time was at hand and that the return of Jesus Christ was now imminent—the countdown for Christ's return had begun!

The opening of the **Seventh Seal** will serve as a warning **to the world** that the final end-time tribulation has come and that the return of Jesus Christ is now imminent—the final countdown for Christ's return has begun!

There was great spiritual tribulation upon the Church during the opening of the first four seals. Two-thirds of the Church went by the wayside during the first few months of this devastation. The details of this event are in the pages of *The Prophesied End-Time.*

Although the remaining third of the Church was shaken bitterly by these events, it was scattered, nevertheless, into several hundred, separate, feuding organizations. The Church had strayed far away from the spiritual application of God's way of love that brother should live toward brother. The love of many had waxed cold among God's own people, just as Jesus Christ said it would (Matthew 24:12). God's Church, small by the world's perspective, was scattered throughout the world and no longer in unity as one true Church.

The first three seals allowed for the self-destruction of two-thirds of God's own Church, as a result of her pride, sin and spiritual lukewarmness.

The period of the Fourth Seal was a prophetic revelation of what would occur to the remaining third of the Church that was scattered. Since this last third would not repent of its guilt in causing the devastating results from the opening of the first three seals, the Church began to fall asleep once again and experience a repetition of the same kind of destruction as in the first three seals. During this same time, God began to chasten, mold and fashion a remnant of that last third, through whom He would finish His work in this last era of the Church.

God has been very specific about His remnant at the end. At present, that remnant is only about a tenth, a tithe, of what God said He would stir and awaken. This book will help serve as a tool to awaken the remaining ninety percent (which will then constitute ten percent of the last third of the Church that was scattered). God's Church eagerly awaits those who will be awakened and returned to Him.

Of that last third of the Church that was scattered, ninety percent will not be awakened by God before Christ's return and will not have opportunity to enter the millennial era that follows. Instead, the period of the Fourth Seal served as a warning that this scattered third would experience a similar devastation as the first two-thirds did.

Right now, what happened to the Church during the first four seals may not mean much to you; but it is vitally important due to a prophetic duality concerning great physical destruction (tribulation) on the world, and very specifically, upon the United States.

Just as the Church was caught off guard, even though God gave it warning, the world will be caught off guard, even though God will have given it warning. When the Seventh Seal is opened, the physical type of duality will begin just as the spiritual type was first accomplished upon God's Church in the opening of the first four seals.

At the opening of the Seventh Seal, the fulfillment of a physical duality will begin exactly when devastation strikes the United States first. This country is the focus for the beginning of great tribulation which will strike the earth in the final three and one-half years that precede the return of Jesus Christ, when He takes over the rule of all government on the earth. One-third of this nation will be destroyed at the onset. But before we cover the Seventh Seal, let's back up to address the previous seal.

Opening the Seals

There are Seven Seals in the Book of Revelation to be opened at the end-time. As mentioned, the first five seals pertained to God's Church. The timing for the opening of the seals has always been in God, the Father's, sole care and control. The Book of Revelation shows that there is only one whom God said was worthy to open these seals:

> *I* [John] *saw in the right hand of Him who sat upon the throne a scroll written within and on the backside, sealed with seven seals* [a scroll of the Seven Seals of Revelation]. *And I saw a strong angel proclaiming with a loud voice, "Who is worthy to open the book, and to undo its seals?" And no one in heaven, nor on earth, neither under the earth, was able to open the book, neither to look thereon. And I wept much because no one was found worthy to open and to read the book, neither to look thereon.*
> (Revelation 5:1-4)

God gave countless prophecies to His prophets about the end-time, but the full meaning of those prophecies was not to be revealed until the very last few years of man's allotted 6,000 years of self-rule. The prophet Daniel wrote many things concerning this end-time, yet no one has understood the full meaning of those end-time prophecies because, like the Seven Seals of Revelation, God purposed not to reveal the specific meaning until the end. However, many people have tried to explain what these prophecies mean, even though it has always been God's purpose to keep them closed—veiled—until the end-time. This is that time, and that is the very reason God has raised up a prophet to reveal what has, until now, been sealed!

Daniel wanted to know the meaning of what he had written concerning the end-time, but notice what God told him. *"Go your way Daniel because these words are **closed up** and **sealed** until the end-time"* (Daniel 12:9).

Notice what John was told when he was weeping because he could see no one who was found worthy to open the Seven Seals:

> *And one of the elders* [one of God's twenty-four elders] *said unto me, "Don't weep, but behold the Lion of the tribe of Judah, the Root of David* [Jesus Christ]*, has prevailed **to open** the book and **to undo** the seven seals thereof."* (Revelation 5:5)

The twenty-four elders then began to sing a song addressing Jesus Christ:

> *You are worthy to take the book, and to open the seals thereof, for you were slain and have redeemed* <u>*them*</u> [the 144,000 who will return with Christ] *to God, by your blood, out of every kindred, and tongue, and people, and nation. And you have made* <u>*them*</u> *unto our God kings and priests, and* <u>*they*</u> *shall reign upon the earth.* (Revelation 5:9-10)

In His own time, God gave Jesus Christ the responsibility of opening the Seven Seals. When Christ began to open those seals, He revealed their meaning to me, His servant, one of God's end-time prophets. The meaning of specific end-time events and their actual occurrence on earth could not be known until Christ began to open the seals.

Again, six seals have already been opened; only one remains.

DIVISION OF THE SEVEN SEALS

Sixth Seal contains Seven Thunders.
  Seventh Seal is divided into Seven Trumpets.
     Seventh Trumpet is divided into Seven Last Plagues.

The **Sixth Seal** (the current period at the time of this writing) has **Seven Thunders** that sound intermittently throughout this period, growing louder, even as they continue into the period of the Seventh Seal.

There are **Seven Seals** of the Book of Revelation that are opened by Jesus Christ. The **Seventh Seal** itself **is divided into** seven distinct periods of great physical destruction unleashed on the earth, and these events are announced by the sounding of **Seven Trumpets.** The last three of the Seven Trumpets are also referred to as the Three Last Woes. The Seventh Trumpet sounds on the final day of the last three and one-half years of great tribulation, and this **Seventh Trumpet** itself is **divided into the Seven Last Plagues.**

The Sixth Seal

We are, right now, in the time period of the Sixth Seal with only one seal remaining to be opened. This book is being written toward the end of this period of time. There isn't much time left before the Seventh Seal will be opened and the last three and one-half years of man's rule will be brought to a close. This prophetic time, which is recorded throughout the Bible, is described as the worst time of destruction and death the earth has ever witnessed.

Before that last seal is opened, you need to know what is happening now, and why, so that you can come to understand what you must do to better prepare for what is coming next.

This current time, within the duration of the Sixth Seal, is a time of transition between events that specifically concern the Church of God (the completion of a spiritual phase) and the prophetic events that are beginning to unfold (to be unveiled) in physical destruction on the earth (the beginning of a physical phase). This is the period of time of escalating physical destruction, which is best depicted as a pregnant woman in labor pains.

The period of the Sixth Seal is of great meaning to God because during this time He will complete a work that He has been doing throughout the past 6,000 years. During those millennia, God has been preparing His own government that will rule this earth after the return of Jesus Christ. Throughout the entirety of the past 6,000 years, God has been continuously calling those whom He would prepare to be part of that government, those who will reign with Jesus Christ when His Kingdom comes to take control of all rulership over the earth. Before that Seventh Seal can be opened, this great work of God must first be finished.

When the Seventh Seal is opened, Seven Trumpets will sound consecutively, each one announcing a new phase of destruction. The sounding of the first four trumpets primarily concerns the demise of the United States, although other countries are also going to suffer mightily at this same time. John spoke of this time:

> *And when He* [Jesus Christ] *had opened the seventh seal, there was silence in heaven about the space of half an hour. And I* [John] *saw the seven angels which stood before God, and to them were given seven trumpets.* (Revelation 8:1-2)

This will be covered more thoroughly later, but this account is the beginning of the description of those seven angels to whom the seven trumpets have been given. When they sound their trumpets, very specific events of horribly destructive power will be unleashed upon the earth. But it needs to be noted here that the first four trumpets announce massive destruction, which is first and foremost upon the United States and her closest allies.

These first four trumpets of the Seventh Seal have been mentioned so that you can better understand the flow of events which unfold during the Sixth Seal. Now, for a more complete picture, let's back up and notice what is said to these first four angels of the Seventh Seal before they are allowed to sound their trumpets, which result in the demise of the United States:

> *And I* [John] *saw another angel ascending from the east, having the seal of the living God, and he cried with a loud voice to the four angels, to whom it was given to hurt the earth and the sea* [the angels with the first four trumpets of the Seventh Seal]*, saying, "Hurt not the earth, neither the sea, nor the trees, until we have sealed the servants of our God in their foreheads." And I heard the number of them who were sealed, and there were sealed an hundred*

and forty-four thousand of all the tribes of the children of Israel. (Revelation 7:2-4)

John saw this angel, who is pictured as the one who carries God's seal that is to be set upon those who are to be part of God's Kingdom. This angel has a job to complete, and he has a message to the first four angels of the Seventh Seal. He told those four angels that they must wait until his job is completed before they could begin to sound their trumpets.

Those Being Sealed

Who are these 144,000 who are to receive God's seal, and what does this mean? There have been numerous theological ideas about who this 144,000 might be, but as always, man's religion is wrong.

The problem with man's religion is that he does not understand the purpose and plan that God is working out on this earth. The refusal of religious scholars to be truthful with these verses has only helped to keep traditional Christianity in darkness.

Much of the problem with scholars is that they believe **now** is the time that God is desperately trying to save the world. By this and other false presumptions, they picture God as being very weak and somewhat powerless to save mankind. This is a damnable perversion of what is true. God is Almighty! In this world's theology, Satan is shown as being more powerful than God, since he is pictured as keeping most of the world away from worshiping God. This shows the depth of the blindness that theologians and Biblical scholars have because God is not at work trying to save the world at this time. As this book will show, God's awesome plan of salvation, that is to be offered to all mankind, is far beyond the grasp of scholars and theologians to understand.

Today, without exception, **every** theologian and scholar of the Bible is fully blind to the truths of God. This is part of the mess that God is getting ready to correct through His two end-time witnesses. God is going to make a clear distinction between what is true and what is false—who is true and who is a liar!

The truth is: God has not called or worked with very many people over the past 6,000 years. Even in the time of Jesus Christ, only a few believed the truths of God, and most certainly the scholars and religious teachers were not among them. There were thousands of Pharisees and Sadducees, but they did not believe God. They preached about God and those things contained in the writings of the law and prophets, but they did not believe what God said. The same problem exists today. Many preach about God, Jesus Christ and love, but they do not believe God.

There are some scriptures that mention two occasions when a few thousand did come out to hear Jesus Christ, but even He explained that they did not do so for the right reasons. On many occasions people stopped following Him because of what He said. John tells of such an account when Jesus spoke of the importance of the symbolism that His sacrifice would have on the fulfillment of the yearly Passover:

> *Then Jesus said unto them, "Truly, truly, I say to you, except you eat the flesh of the Son of man and drink his blood, you have no life in you. Whoever eats my flesh and drinks my blood has eternal life; and I will raise him up at the last day. For, my flesh is meat indeed and my blood is drink indeed. He who eats my flesh and drinks my blood dwells in me, and I in him."* (John 6:53-56)

Jesus explained a spiritual matter that they could not yet understand. He told them about the symbolism that the Church would later picture in the observance of the annual Passover service. This annual service, which God commands His people to partake of year by year, includes a ceremony that consists of eating a piece of unleavened bread and taking a drink of wine. This symbolism concerns the beaten body and spilled blood of Jesus Christ, whereby man can be saved. But many of those Jews who were following Him could not receive His words because, to them, it was unthinkable and against God's health laws that one should eat human flesh or drink blood. So it says, *"From that time, many of his disciples went away and walked no more with him"* (John 6:66).

Sadly, even today the world does not grasp the meaning of this account. Much of traditional Christianity has twisted this into an observance they call Communion. But Jesus Christ spoke of the great meaning His death would fulfill in God's purpose and revelation contained in the annual observance of Passover. Judaism and traditional Christianity refuse God's Passover. Therefore, they remain blind to God's true plan and purpose that is being worked out on this earth.

Judaism refuses to observe Passover on the day God commands, choosing rather to observe their traditional Seder, which they claim is on Passover. Traditional Christianity observes Easter and Communion, but they do not obey the keeping of the annual Passover that even the apostle Paul makes clear should be observed by the Church.

Throughout the three and one-half years of His ministry and up until the time Jesus Christ was killed by the "religious people" of His day (through the Romans), many stopped following Him. It is recorded in the first chapter of Acts, after Christ's death, that Peter addressed only 120 disciples who had remained faithful.

When the Church began on the day of Pentecost, God performed a great miracle to magnify the occasion; yet it was still

His purpose to keep this on a small scale. About three thousand people were moved to repent that day and become part of the Church. Three thousand is still small compared to all those who lived at that time. God's purpose wasn't to have millions become part of His Church at that time. Only a few thousand were called and worked with by God for the great purpose He would manifest at the return of Jesus Christ.

The Church did grow, but it did not grow in the way that most believe. It always remained very small. The Bible speaks of many occasions when people met together in homes. Homes were small and the Church was small.

Traditional Christianity has pictured the Church as growing larger through time until today, when it believes the Church has grown into the millions. **This is not true!** This has not been God's purpose. The Church of God has always been small—even today. And what is the reason? For 6,000 years God has been "handpicking" those who are to become part of a world ruling government at the return of Jesus Christ. God has a plan of salvation, but it is not one that the world teaches! You have exciting things yet to learn about life and death and how **all** people are going to be given opportunity for salvation, an opportunity that has not been given during the past 6,000 years.

So, who are those 144,000 being sealed by God? They are those who, throughout the past six millennia, God has specifically chosen to mold and fashion so that they could one day be given life again, in order to rule in His Kingdom at the return of Jesus Christ.

During the first four thousand years of human history, God worked with a very few to become part of that new government in His Kingdom. This should be easy for people to see when they read the Old Testament. Not many are mentioned as following God and being worked with by Him.

Even in the beginning, after several hundred years, Noah is mentioned as only the eighth preacher of righteousness. Over 4,000 years, not many were called by God.

When Abram and Sarai (whose names were later changed to Abraham and Sarah) were first called, no one else was being worked with by God. There were other several hundred-year periods when only a handful of people were worked with by God.

Six million people were delivered from the oppression of Pharaoh in Egypt. God worked with only a few of them in a spiritual manner, during forty years in the wilderness, for the purpose of becoming part of His future government.

It wasn't until Pentecost in 31 A.D., when the Church began, that God started to work with larger numbers of people, but the numbers were still very small in comparison to religions that called themselves "of God." Over the past 2,000 years, God has used the organized environment of His Church and His trained ministry to work with larger numbers of people. But when all is said and done, only 144,000 people, in six millennia of human history, will have received the seal of God, enabling them to become part of His government that will reign on the earth.

It will be at the return of Jesus Christ that God's Kingdom will come to rule the earth—immediately after man's self-rule has been brought to a complete and final end. The coming of His government is the focus of the beginning of the outline of prayer that Jesus Christ gave His disciples when they asked Him how to pray:

> *This is the manner after which you should pray: Our Father who is in heaven, let your name be sanctified.* ***Your Kingdom come . . .*** (Matthew 6:9-10)

God's Coming Government

God's purpose from the outset, before He ever placed man on earth, was to give him 6,000 years of self-rule before He would step in and bring to a close the great lesson from that entire period—man cannot rule himself. The true witness of man's history is that he has consistently rejected God and His ways, and the consequence is that he has been unable to successfully rule himself. This is the greatest lesson that can be learned from man's time on earth.

In the beginning, God established the seven-day week. The week is a prophetic type for the timing that God would use to work out His purpose for mankind. Just as there are seven days in the week, God has a plan of 7,000 years for mankind.

Six days were given to man to go about his own business, but the seventh day was God's time: a time that man was to acknowledge as the day that was set apart by God. In turn, man was to obey God and set apart the seventh-day Sabbath for religious observance. The world has done a miserable job of obeying this instruction from God. Most of traditional Christianity has moved its time for worshipping God to the same time God condemned throughout the Old Testament writings. That time was when Israel worshiped Baal and Moloch (gods of the sun) on the first day of the week—Sunday. Is it any wonder the world remains blind to the true ways of God?

Just as God gave man six days to do his own work, God gave man 6,000 years of self-rule. The true witness is that man has failed to successfully rule himself. Man's greatest attempt to establish peace in modern times is the United Nations. This institution, during a time of the greatest technology and advanced education ever, is man's greatest witness yet that man has failed.

We have come to the end of God's allotted time for man's self-rule, the end of 6,000 years of man; and now, the next 1,000 years will be God's time as pictured by the prophetic seven-day week (the first six days coming to an end and the next day—the seventh—being God's time). It is time for God's rule to be established on earth, but unlike this present time, man will no longer be able to deceive others concerning the correct time to observe God's Sabbath. Man will no longer be able to deceive others concerning what is true in the next 1,000 years because God's Kingdom **will** be established and His government **will** rule this whole earth. There will be no other religion on earth—only the true Church of God. There will be no other government on earth—only the reign of the Kingdom of God.

The 144,000

For six millennia God has been working with each individual who will be part of the structure of His new government that is about to be established. Jesus Christ will be the head of that new government and the 144,000, whom God has chosen and trained, will be resurrected to serve in that government.

So who are the 144,000? Although the number is not given in Revelation 5, these are the same ones mentioned earlier when it was shown that Jesus Christ was the only one that God revealed was worthy to open the Seals of Revelation. The twenty-four elders spoke of Jesus Christ being worthy to open the seals:

> *You are worthy to take the book, and to open the seals thereof, for you were slain and have redeemed them* [the 144,000] *to God, by your blood, out of every kindred, and tongue, and people, and nation. And you have made them unto our God kings and priests, and they shall **reign upon the earth**."* (Revelation 5:9-10)

These are the ones whom God has molded and fashioned throughout the space of six millennia. There is only one group of people who have been redeemed through time who will be resurrected at the return of Jesus Christ.

The Book of Revelation was not written so that it could be understood by anyone who read it. Although John wrote Revelation, the meaning of what he wrote was not revealed even to him. It was written, as the name implies, in such a way that one would require **God's own revelation** to understand it. For the most part, God was not going to reveal the full meaning contained in it until the time that the Seals began to be opened—when they were no longer sealed.

People who read Revelation become entangled in misinterpretations because the Seals have been mostly concealed (except in some very basic ways to God's own Church).

Such is the case of the 144,000. There will be only one great resurrection on the very day that Jesus Christ returns, and this will be the 144,000. There will be no others! This same group of people is referred to in different ways throughout Revelation, but it is always the one and selfsame group.

When reading Revelation 7, most people believe two separate groups of people are being discussed; but they are the same. Let's review the first part of that chapter once again:

> *And I* [John] *saw another angel ascending from the east, having the seal of the living God, and he cried with a loud voice to the four angels, to whom it was given to hurt the earth and the sea* [the angels with the first four trumpets of the Seventh Seal], *saying, "Hurt not the earth, neither the sea, nor the trees, until we have sealed the servants of our God in their foreheads." And I heard the number of them who were sealed, and there were sealed an hundred*

and forty-four thousand of all the tribes of the children of Israel. (Revelation 7:2-4)

For six millennia, the seal of God's approval has been placed upon those whom God has molded and fashioned to become part of His future government. Most who will be in that new government have already been sealed, died and are awaiting the resurrection at Christ's return. There are a very few (still living) who will complete the total makeup of God's new government.

The angel, who carried the instruction from God to the first four angels of the Seventh Seal, told them that they could not begin to sound their trumpets until his job was finished. This angel sets the seal of God upon those whom God has finished training and made ready to serve in His new government. As of this very moment, there are some now living, whom God has finished training, who have been sealed. There are a very few others who are yet to complete that training, and as soon as they have, then they too will be sealed. When that sealing is complete, then the entire 144,000 will be sealed. Then, the Seventh Seal will be opened, and those four angels, who had been restrained, will blow their trumpets. The result will lead to the demise of the United States.

This same angel, who set the seal of God on those who finished their training, announced the total number of all those whom God would seal—144,000. John heard that number and recorded what he heard. Later in the same chapter, John is given a vision of this same group. Notice how he describes it:

After this [This was after John had been told about this 144,000 whom God divided into twelve organizational groups of 12,000 each.] *I looked, and before me there was a great multitude which no man could number, of all nations, kindreds, and people, and tongues, stood before the throne, and before the Lamb, clothed with white robes and palms in their hands.* (Revelation 7:9)

This time, John **was shown** this large number, and he described it as a great multitude. Man is incapable of looking out over such a large multitude and counting it, and man does not have the ability to know the number of people God has prepared through time. Only God knows all those whom He has prepared and sealed. God had to reveal this to man. So in the beginning of this chapter, He **told the number** to John.

Then one of the twenty-four elders of God asked John a question:

Who are these who are clothed in white robes and from where do they come? And I [John] *said, "Sir, you know." Then he said to me, "These are those who came out of great tribulation, and they have washed their robes and made them white in the blood of the Lamb"* (Revelation 7:13-14).

As with the same group mentioned in Revelation 5, these are also described as being redeemed by the blood of the Passover Lamb—Jesus Christ. These have been called by God from among people throughout the world, through time. Their training has been difficult, and they have battled to change their nature in order to yield to God's will, rather than their own. This conquering process is described as coming out of great tribulation.

By not understanding the structure of God's new government, some have believed that the great multitude described in the last half of Revelation 7 is a different group from those 144,000 described in the first half. In addition, since the 144,000 are further broken down into twelve groups of 12,000, with each bearing the name of one of the twelve tribes of Israel, some have believed that this meant that these people were literally—physically—of these twelve tribes. This is not true.

God's Design

As described in the New Testament, God is going to offer salvation to the entirety of mankind, not to Judah only. Salvation is not about the physical people of Israel; it is for the spiritual Israel of God—the Church of God. Eventually, in God's plan, everyone will be given opportunity to become part of the Church of God, through which they can grow and mature until they are able to enter the Kingdom of God. God's Kingdom is spiritual and composed entirely of spirit beings who have been given the gift of eternal life. The structure of God's Family bears the name of Israel, which means "God prevails."

God's Family is one that He molds and fashions. As with everything God creates, there is awesome organization, design, structure, and complete order that is established through His will. God's overall design and structure for His Kingdom is that it will bear the name of Israel, but it is also divided into twelve specific segments of operation, with each bearing one of the names of the tribes of Israel.

God inspired John to write about this spiritual structure through a type which can be seen in a physical manner. The very structure of God's Kingdom is described in terms of a holy city—new Jerusalem:

> *And he* [an angel] *carried me away in the spirit to a great and high mountain, and showed me that great city, the holy Jerusalem, descending out of heaven from God, having the glory of God. Her light was like that of a most precious stone, even like a jasper stone which is clear as crystal. It had a great wall that was very high, and it had*

twelve gates, and at the gates twelve angels, and names were written on each gate, which are the names of the twelve tribes of the children of Israel: on the east three gates; on the north three gates; on the south three gates; and on the west three gates. (Revelation 21:10-13)

John saw what was given to him in a physical representation of what is actually a type of the spiritual structure and organization of God's new Kingdom. There are additional descriptions that show more of the design of God and the importance of His use of twelve in it. God's organization is a literal structure that is spiritual in design. God has chosen names to describe various parts of His organization. Even the names of the twelve apostles of Christ will be used in that structure, *"And the wall of the city had twelve foundations, and in them the names of the twelve apostles of the Lamb"* (Revelation 21:14).

The division of the 144,000 into twelve groups, with each bearing the name of one of the tribes of Israel, is spiritual in composition and does not mean that this number is derived from people who are literally from those physical tribes.

There is one more area where the number of 144,000 is described. As we have read in Revelation 7, God simply gave John the exact number that He would seal over six millennia—those who would comprise His new government. In the second half of that chapter, John was given a vision of that great multitude. The other account, that mentions this group by number, is the occasion in which a sequence of end-time events leads to the time of the actual resurrection of all 144,000 on the very day of Christ's second coming to this earth:

Then I looked and beheld a Lamb who stood on Mount Zion, and with Him an hundred forty and four thousand who had His Father's name written in their forehead.

And I heard a voice from heaven, as the voice of many waters, and as the voice of loud thunder, and I heard the sound of harpists playing their harps. They sang as it were a new song before the throne, before the four living creatures, and the elders. No one could learn that song except the hundred and forty-four thousand who were redeemed from the earth. These are the ones who were not defiled with women, for they are virgins [spiritual]. *These are the ones who follow the Lamb wherever He goes. These were redeemed from among men, being firstfruits to God and to the Lamb.* (Revelation 14:1-4)

Those who are shown as returning with Jesus Christ on this very last day of man's allotted time for self-rule are also referred to throughout the Bible as God's firstfruits. The reason for this is that of all who have lived throughout time, these are the first to enter God's Family—the first to be given eternal life in the Kingdom of God.

The Reign of God's Government

Time has run out for man, and the time has come for God's government to be established. Yes, all end-time events described throughout the Book of Revelation mark the end of man's self-rule and the beginning of God's rule.

The very last day of man's self-rule—the last day of the three and one-half years of great tribulation—is marked by powerful events. The events of that day will be described in more detail in another chapter, but it is important to note the power of this transition—from man's world to God's.

That last day is described as the day of God's great wrath upon those who have been destroying the earth over the previous few years. Much of Europe and large portions of Russia, China and other Eastern countries will be destroyed on this day. It is exactly at this point that God will step in to prevent mankind from destroying himself because it is at this very time that two great armies will have come together to confront each other in a final, all-out battle for supremacy. These armies, numbering over two hundred million, will be completely destroyed in that one day.

It will be on this last day that all 144,000, who will reign in God's new government—in the Kingdom of God, will be resurrected. They will reign on this earth with Jesus Christ for 1,000 years.

Let's notice how some of these events are described. John is describing some of what he saw on this last day:

I saw heaven opened, and behold a white horse, and He who sat upon him was called Faithful and True, and in righteousness He does judge and make war. His eyes were as a flame of fire, and on His head were many crowns, and He had a name written that no man knew, but He Himself. He was clothed with a vesture dipped in blood, and His name is called The Word of God [He is Jesus Christ]. *And the armies which were in heaven* [the 144,000 who had just been resurrected] *followed Him upon white horses, and they were clothed in fine linen, white and clean* [the description given to those redeemed by God over six millennia]. *And out of His mouth went a sharp sword, that with it He should smite the nations, and He shall rule them with a rod of iron* [This will bring an end to man's government and establish God's] *He treads the winepress of the fierceness and wrath of Almighty God. He has on His vesture and on His thigh a name written, KING OF KINGS, AND LORD OF LORDS.* (Revelation 19:11-16)

As was stated in Revelation 5, those redeemed from among mankind over six millennia are made kings and priests unto God. They will reign with Jesus Christ for 1,000 years in this new government that God has sent to the earth. Revelation 20 continues on to describe this army of 144,000 that has returned with Jesus Christ:

> *And I saw thrones, and they* [the 144,000] *sat upon them, and judgment was given unto them, and I saw the souls of them that were cutoff* [from the world] *for the witness of Jesus, and for the word of God, and who had not worshipped the beast, neither his image, neither had received his mark upon their foreheads, or in their hands. They lived and **reigned with Christ a thousand years**. But the rest of the dead* [all of mankind who had lived on earth over six millennia and were dead by the time of this last day] *lived not again until the thousand years were finished* [the great resurrection to be explained later]. *This is the first resurrection* [that of the 144,000] *Blessed and holy is he that has part in the first resurrection because on such the second death hath no power* [because they are resurrected to immortal—eternal life], *and they shall be priests of God and of Christ, and they shall reign with Him a thousand years.* (Revelation 20:4-6)

On this final day of man's self-rule, when Jesus Christ returns, God will bring an end to all remaining governments on earth. By doing so, the way will be made ready for His government to be established. Finally, after six millennia of man's miserable self-rule, his governments and religions will be brought to a close. Finally, the time will have come for a new world to be established under the righteous reign of Jesus Christ. Man's reign has been far from righteous! The beauty and glory of a world under God's government will have to be experienced because man cannot conceive of the richness and fullness of such a life.

The Transition of the Sixth Seal

As was explained earlier, at this present time (of this writing) we are in the period of time that makes up the Sixth Seal. Actually, we are in the latter half of that period. The duration of the Sixth Seal is a time of transition between events that specifically concern the Church of God (the completion of a spiritual phase) and the prophetic events that are beginning to unfold (to be unveiled) in greater physical destruction on the earth (the beginning of a physical phase).

This chapter has explained the first portion of this transition which includes God's primary work concerning the purpose of His Church. For nearly 6,000 years, God has been calling and training 144,000 people to comprise His soon-coming world government. All 144,000 will be resurrected on the last day of man's self-rule on earth. They will meet Jesus Christ at His return. It will be on this last day that the Kingdom of God will be established on earth to reign over all mankind for the next 1,000 years.

This great work of God over six millennia is nearly complete! Once this work has been finished (the spiritual phase complete), the Seventh Seal will be opened. The duration of the Sixth Seal is a time of transition between the completion of a spiritual phase and the beginning of a physical phase for the fulfillment of end-time prophecies. The transition of both phases is coordinated to lead into the opening of the Seventh Seal.

The physical phase of transition that is occurring during this present Sixth Seal is the period when prophetic end-time events escalate, on a physical plane, with increasing destructive power that is best depicted as a pregnant woman in labor pains. But there is more to this phase of transition that will lead to the opening of the Seventh Seal and the destruction that will come at the blowing of the first four trumpets. This second phase of physical transition, which is the beginning of prophetic end-time destruction, will be addressed in the next chapter.

Chapter 4

THE SEVEN THUNDERS OF THE 6TH SEAL

In the last chapter, it was shown that the Sixth Seal is a transitional period. It concludes the spiritual phase of God's plan to finish His work of final training and sealing of those few, still living, who will be added to complete the 144,000 and be in His new government. This is an awesome thing! For six millennia God has been molding and preparing a government to rule in righteousness over all the earth for 1,000 years.

As we approach the end of this spiritual phase of God's work, a physical phase of destruction has begun in the world. It is steadily increasing in frequency and magnitude. This escalating destruction, throughout the world, is a forewarning of far greater destruction to follow once the Seventh Seal is opened. Before the horror of that final worldwide destruction strikes the earth, you have a short time in which you can heed the warnings of this book and respond to God in an appropriate manner (if the Seventh Seal has not been opened by the time you read this).

The sooner people respond to God, the better prepared they can be for what lies ahead; and most important of all, they will be more likely to receive favor and help from God. However, it is important to understand two vital points. God does not owe favor or help to anyone, therefore it is wise to seek Him early, and in a genuine spirit, so that He might have mercy upon you.

Secondly, everyone on earth will experience some suffering through the destructive times that are just ahead. Those who do not have God's favor will experience great suffering and most will die. Therefore, to survive the most difficult time in all human history, it would be wise to seek God's favor and help early if you want to have opportunity to live into a new world of wonderful prosperity and righteous government.

By contrast, the governments of man are filled with lies, corruption, special interests, excessive taxation, bloated bureaucracy, oppression, red tape, favoritism, injustice, bickering, fighting, war mongering, selfishness, egotism, pride, thirst for money and power, and on it goes! Can you imagine a one-world government that is void of such oppressiveness and pettiness—a government that is genuinely "for the people?"

The destructive escalation during this physical phase of the Sixth Seal has been likened to a pregnant woman who is in labor pain. God is going to show that there is more to this process, written about in Revelation, that has never been revealed until now.

The Seven Thunders

Not only did God close up the meaning and timing for the events of the Seven Seals of Revelation until they were to be revealed in this prophetic end-time, but He also told John not to write about what he heard concerning the Seven Thunders. God wanted the Seven Thunders to remain sealed until this very time as well.

God did all this as part of a process through which He would reveal who one of His end-time witnesses was, the one through whom He would fully reveal all that John had written in the Book of Revelation concerning this end-time. God gave specific end-time prophecies to John in a vision. John was to write about what he saw, but most of what he wrote was to remain sealed. God predetermined to reveal the meaning and timing of these major prophetic events through His end-time prophet.

God has a twofold purpose for doing this. First, God is going to make a clear distinction, in His scattered Church, between who His true minister is, through whom He is working, and all other ministers with whom He is not working. This will serve as one final witness to the Church before the devastation of the great tribulation strikes the whole world at the opening of the Seventh Seal.

Secondly, God's other purpose, for revealing this prophecy in this manner, is to make a clear distinction among all religious leaders in this world. God is going to reveal who His true minister is, through whom He is working to proclaim His truth to the world as a final end-time witness, and He will begin to reveal who all the false religious leaders are.

The timing for the Seven Thunders is during the period of the Sixth Seal. Let's notice what John wrote:

> *And I saw another mighty angel come down out of the heaven, clothed with a cloud, and a rainbow was on his head, and his face was like the sun, and his feet as pillars of fire. He had a little book open in his hand, and he set his right foot on the sea and his left foot on the land, and cried with a loud voice, as when a lion roars. When he had cried, the seven thunders uttered their sounds. And when the seven thunders had uttered their sounds, I was about to write, but I heard a voice from heaven saying to me, "Seal up those things which the seven thunders uttered, and do not write them." The angel whom I saw standing on the sea and on the land lifted up his hand to*

heaven, and swore by Him who lives for ever and ever, who created heaven and the things that are in it, the earth and the things that are in it, and the sea and the things that are in it, that there should be time no longer. But in the days of the voice of the seventh angel **[the angel of the Seventh Trumpet of the Seventh Seal]**, *when he shall begin to sound, the mystery of God shall be finished, as He has declared to his servants the prophets. Then the voice which I heard from heaven spoke to me again and said, "Go and take the little book which is open in the hand of the angel who stands on the sea and on the earth." So I went to the angel and said to him, "Give me the little book." And he said to me, "Take it and eat it, and it will make your belly bitter, but it will be sweet as honey in your mouth." Then I took the little book out of the angel's hand and ate it, and it was like honey in my mouth, and as soon as I ate it, my belly was made bitter. And he said to me, "You must prophesy again before many peoples, and nations, and tongues, and kings."* (Revelation 10:1-11)

What does all this mean? Simply reading this does not tell you anything specific. It was not written so that just anyone reading it could understand. For that matter, none of the Book of Revelation was written so that just anyone reading it could understand. It has to be revealed through God's servants, and most of it was reserved to be revealed at this end-time through God's end-time prophet—**me**.

Hopefully you will not make the error that so many do when reading such a bold statement by simply dismissing it because of the way it sounds. Such a statement can understandably sound brazen (brash), but it is not. It is simply a reality, and it is my job and responsibility to clearly speak in these terms. Before I tell you what the Seven Thunders are, there is something that you must be reminded of first.

Amidst all the horrifying events that will unfold from this point forward, until the end-time tribulation is over and Jesus Christ finally returns, God will tell the world what is happening and why there is such devastation. God will even tell these things in advance. How will He do this? He will do it through His end-time prophets—His two witnesses, but He will do it primarily through me, His end-time spokesman.

To be reminded of what these two witnesses will be doing during the final three and one-half years of great worldwide tribulation, a paragraph in the first chapter of this book needs to be repeated here:

> Later, in the Book of Revelation, God gives symbolism that reflects the importance of His two witnesses. Notice what God says, *"And I will give power unto my two witnesses, and they shall prophesy a thousand two hundred and sixty days, clothed in sackcloth* [symbolic of humility]. *These are the two olive trees, and the two lamp stands <u>standing</u>* [Gk.—set, established] <u>*before*</u> [Gk.—in the presence of] *the God of the earth"* (Revelation 11:3-4). A literal translation of this verse is saying, "These are the two olive trees and the two lamp stands which are established in the presence of God unto the earth." These two people are represented as two lamp stands and two olive trees which God sets before Him to reveal His will to the whole earth.

The verses that follow these have not yet been quoted. They reveal more about the role of these two witnesses during that last three and one-half years:

And if any man will hurt them, fire proceeds out of their mouth and devours their enemies, and if any man will hurt them, he must in this manner be killed. They have power to shut heaven so that it does not rain in the days of their prophecy, and they have power over waters to turn them to blood, and to smite the earth with all plagues, as often as they will. (Revelation 11:5-6)

God is revealing that some will hate these two witnesses so much that they will try to do them bodily harm, even trying to kill them. But God makes it clear, as already explained, that these two people will not die until God allows it. They will be killed in Jerusalem just three and one-half days prior to the return of Jesus Christ.

The fire proceeding out of their mouth is symbolic of the power to pronounce exacting judgments upon anyone who would do them harm. Whatever the two witnesses pronounce will come to pass. If people try to kill them (two witnesses), the very manner in which they seek to accomplish this will be the very manner in which they will die. God will give divine protection to His two witnesses. He will give them great power to not only pronounce how some will suffer for trying to do them harm, but God will also give them power to perform devastating destruction **as often as they choose**. They will be given power beyond that which Moses was given when he led the Israelites out of Egypt. They, too, will be able to turn the waters to blood. They will be able to close up the heavens so that it will not rain on any area they choose. They will have power to call all manner of plagues upon any part of the earth as often as they choose.

God will reveal who His two witnesses are regardless of whether people choose to believe them or not! God will increasingly give more proof of His spokesman as prophecies unfold exactly as they are recorded in this book. When the Seventh Seal is opened, the first four trumpets of that seal will announce the final demise of the United States and her closest allies. The opening of this seal will be the beginning of the final three and one-half years of great worldwide tribulation. Before we cover those events, which are the subject of another chapter, we need to look more closely at the events that precede the last seal, events which are pronounced by Seven Thunders during the time of the Sixth Seal.

Thunder perfectly describes what is happening before the final end-time storm of destruction strikes this earth. The final storm will engulf the whole earth for three and one-half years, but as that storm approaches, the rumbling of this thunder will be heard with increasing intensity.

These Seven Thunders parallel another prophetic analogy that describes this time of the Sixth Seal. This prophetic period was described earlier as a pregnant woman in labor pain. This analogy is magnified in the revelation of the Seven Thunders.

The Seven Thunders will be declared in the remainder of this chapter. Those thunders have never been announced before now. Everything else that John wrote, concerning the Seven Seals, Seven Trumpets and the Seven Last Plagues, was declared by an angel. The Seven Thunders did not come from angels. John heard the sound of Seven Thunders. It concerned a message about an end-time prophet of God. The specifics of the Seven Thunders were left for this end-time in order to be declared—to be pronounced—by God's end-time prophet, the spokesperson of the two end-time witnesses. More about this will be explained in the Sixth Thunder.

A worldwide storm is brewing, and the warning of that approaching storm is contained in seven distinctive types of thunder. Each thunder will be described, but you need to understand that the thundering is like the pregnant woman in labor pain. All Seven Thunders will increase in intensity as this great end-time storm approaches, but one type of thunder will be more pronounced than another from one great labor pain to another. Each type of thunder will continue to rumble, but at certain times one will be much louder than all the others. Each time that one of the Seven Thunders is much louder (far more pronounced) than all the others is a time that fulfills the prophetic type of a woman in labor pain.

The Seven Thunders have much to do with **how** God will reveal His two witnesses. These thunders serve as a prelude to the final tribulation and the greater manifestation of the two witnesses.

The revelation of the Seven Thunders has everything to do with the revelation of God's end-time witness about man and God's revelation of His two witnesses to man! Sadly, most will **choose** to ignore what they hear.

The First Thunder

September 11, 2001 was a day that thundered so loudly that the very mention of it is recognized all over this world. Mention that day anywhere on earth and people know what happened. However, people do not yet recognize the real meaning behind why this day is so vastly important.

What happened in New York, Washington D.C. and a field in Pennsylvania is not what is most important about this day. What happened on a Biblical plane is of far greater significance!

This date became etched in the minds of people throughout the world, and so did another word. That day began to put the name **al-Qaeda** into the minds of all who had **9/11** written in their memory.

The greater reality for this day is its Biblical significance. The events of this day are prophetic, and the prophetic symbolism of these events is the very thing that will lead to the opening of the Seventh Seal of Revelation and a full blown World War III.

Terrorism and war are not new to mankind. This has been the way of man for thousands of years, but this terrorism is part of end-time prophecy; and this is what makes it different from all other acts of war.

#1:   The **First Thunder** is the beginning **terror of war** for the end-time. This is war that is prophetic for the end-time.

All Seven Thunders contain things that have occurred on the earth in one way or another ever since man's beginning. Terrorism is not new. Wars are not new. But what is happening now, in these Seven Thunders, is new because it is part of end-time prophecy. All these things will lead directly into the final three and one-half years of great physical tribulation on all the earth, with ever increasing intensity.

The success of al-Qaeda's terrorist attack on 9/11 was the beginning of the First Thunder. This was the very day the Sixth Seal of the Book of Revelation was opened. So the events of this day have very great Biblical and prophetic significance!

Terrorism is war and war is terror. An American Civil War General, William T. Sherman, is recognized for a famous quote, in which he said, "War is hell." Anyway you address it, war reigns terror wherever it strikes.

Since 9/11, we have seen more rumblings from the "terror of war." There are continuous rumblings on a lesser scale as al-Qaeda operatives strike at various times and places in the world. However, as time passes, they will strike with far greater power than 9/11. At this time, the beginning rumblings of war are coming from Iran and will lead into greater global terror.

Louder rumblings from the "terror of war" have occurred as a direct response to 9/11. On October 7, 2001, the United States began bombing Afghanistan in what was called Operation Enduring Freedom. In actuality, it stirred up greater resentment and hatred toward Americans, in much of the world, more than it produced the promotion of freedom. Al-Qaeda was dislodged from one part of the world, but its influence and strength has grown much greater since then.

As for Afghanistan, it has successfully returned to its former economic base—being the world's largest producer of illegal opium. Notice the following quote from the Business section of a *BBC News* article dated March 3, 2003:

> Afghanistan retakes heroin crown: Afghanistan retook its place as the world's leading producer of heroin last year, after US-led forces overthrew the Taleban which had banned cultivation of opium poppies. The finding was made in a key drug report, distributed in Kabul on Sunday by the US State Department, which supports almost identical findings by the United Nations last week.

Another great rumbling from this same thunder occurred on March 30, 2003, when the United States began its "Shock and Awe" bombing of Iraq. This was a great "labor pain" because it had a powerful prophetic impact on the attitudes of countries around the world. This moved nations into prophetic alliances, which will become fully realized when WW III begins.

September 11, 2001 is one of the more significant days in end-time prophetic events. It was the day the Sixth Seal of Revelation was opened and the day the First of the Seven Thunders began to sound. The events of this day summarize in prophetic symbolism what is to follow once the Seventh Seal of Revelation is opened—the complete demise of the United States and her closest allies.

The Prophetic Symbolism of 9/11

From the vantage point of all the nations of the world, there could be no greater symbolism of the height of the greatness in wealth, might, and stature of the United States than the World Trade Center towers.

To better understand some of this symbolism, let's consider some of the history about these towers:

> The World Trade Center towers were best known for its iconic 110-story Twin Towers. The towers survived a bombing on February 26, 1993, but all of the original buildings in the complex were destroyed in the September 11, 2001 attacks. Towers One and Two collapsed, and the others (numbers 3, 4, 5, & 6) were damaged beyond repair and later demolished. Building Seven collapsed in the late afternoon on the day of the attacks.

> The towers were initially conceived as a complex dedicated to companies and organizations directly involved in "world trade," but they at first failed to attract the anticipated clientele. During the WTC's early years various governmental organizations became key tenants, yet it was not until the 1980s that the city's perilous

financial state eased, after which an increasing number of private companies—mostly financial firms tied to Wall Street—became tenants.

The towers were best known for its iconic 110-story Twin Towers, but these two towers also served as an icon to the greatness of a nation. Even as the name indicates, they were established upon the ideal of a center for world trade, which the United States has fulfilled for several decades now. The towers were symbolic of the stature of Wall Street itself. The destruction of all seven towers of the World Trade Center, as the destruction of an icon, should not escape Biblical students concerning such symbolism. This is indeed prophetic to the collapse of the United States, which will occur at the opening of the Seventh Seal of Revelation. Such an event should no longer be measured in years, but in months!

The plane that struck the Pentagon in Washington D.C. on the same day should not escape us either. Prophetically, not even the military might of the most powerful nation on earth can escape the judgment of God.

The Second Thunder
There is another rumbling that has been increasing in intensity over the past couple of years. It is the direct result of a marked increase in destructive power being unleashed by the earth itself.

#2:   The **Second Thunder** is the increasing destruction generated by **earthquakes**. Over a period of only two years, there have been over 400,000 deaths from earthquakes with several million additional people being displaced.

The 2004 Indian Ocean earthquake, known by the scientific community as the Sumatra-Andaman earthquake, was an undersea earthquake that occurred on December 26, 2004. According to the United States Geological Survey, the earthquake and its tsunami killed more than 283,100 people, making it one of the deadliest disasters in modern history.

The greatest destruction and loss of life from earthquakes is the direct result of collapsing buildings or the power unleashed in the form of a tsunami. Volcanoes are also associated with earthquakes. All these things will continue to wreak havoc on man and nature in an ever increasing magnitude as we approach the very end of this age.

All Seven Thunders will increase in power and recognition over the next two years (from the date of the first printing of this book) and on into the final three and one-half years of great tribulation. The Seven Thunders will serve as a powerful witness that the words of this book are true, and that they are from the God of Abraham, the Father of Jesus Christ.

The Third Thunder
In terms of an economic impact on property, and even loss of life, one of the most destructive forces that is taking a dramatic turn for the worse is being caused by an escalating change in our weather. Some will argue that the current weather conditions are a reflection of normal cycles of change over time. It is true that the weather follows cycles. Yes, there have always been times of intensity when destructive powers have been unleashed. However, now is different because the destructiveness and change in weather patterns is going to continue to increase dynamically, not following normal patterns.

Some areas will experience abnormally large amounts of rainfall, while others, that normally receive large amounts, will receive none. The consequences of this will be a marked increase in flooding and mudslides in some areas, while other areas will experience growing problems with drought, which as we have seen this past year, results in widespread fires and extensive damage to livestock and crops. Some areas will experience normal amounts of rain, but it will come at the wrong time to benefit agriculture. Too much cold and too much heat at the wrong time will also add to this destructive power. Those who have their livelihood in agriculture have always had to contend with such things, but over the next couple of years these conditions will become the worst yet!

#3   The **Third Thunder** is the growing **destructiveness from weather**.

The record-setting hurricane season of 2005 in the United States has already been mentioned. Experts expected Hurricane Katrina (which hit Alabama, Louisiana and Mississippi on August 29, 2005) to be the costliest natural disaster in U.S. history. Some early estimates exceeded $100 billion, but, as it turns out, the economic impact has exceeded $200 billion.

Just this past week (March 22, 2006), Cyclone Larry (same as a hurricane, except in the northern hemisphere), a Category 5 storm, struck Australia with winds of 180 mph. This incredibly powerful storm went inland about 60 miles south of Cairns. Banana plantations were stripped bare and the damage is expected to run into the hundreds of millions of dollars.

The Fourth Thunder
Each one of the previous prophetic thunders will have an impact

on the fourth thunder. The result of nations fighting terrorism and engaging in war, along with the devastation caused by earthquakes and the destructiveness from weather, will place a greater burden on a crushing global economy.

#4 The **Fourth Thunder** is **global economic upheaval**.

The world is entering into a time of final upheaval for the global economy. The stock market cannot continue its masquerade of being healthy and robust while being falsely propped up by positive talk, pseudo-exuberance and creative forecasting. The day of reckoning is now on the world's doorstep. Many deeply-felt pangs of sickness will reverberate throughout the world as we draw nearer to a huge market crash.

Some nations are already indicating a shift from dollar to euro as a better assurance for future stability. Although many in the United States scoff at such a possibility, that is precisely what will happen as confidence in the dollar continues to wane.

With corporate scandals and corruption on an alarming rise (not to mention never ending downsizing), along with a loss in confidence in a sick economy, the United States is drawing nearer to an economic implosion.

Colorful forecasts, indifferent management, slight-of-hand trickery concerning corporate assets, downsizing, and other corporate gimmickry have reached the point of no return. There will be no bouncing back from the cancerous greed that has nearly choked all life out of free-market capitalism.

Add to all these economic woes the problem of trade deficits, money manipulation, volatile oil markets, and a list of other global ailments; and you have a sure formula for global economic upheaval, the likes of which this world has never seen. The world has experienced times of great economic upheaval, but it has always bounced back in one way or another. This time there will be no bouncing back because the world will experience a complete economic meltdown to a level which not even the hoarding of gold and silver will solve.

The stability of the global economy is on very shaky ground, so much so that even a small country like Iran is making threats that can actually help push it over the edge. This week *World Net Daily* (Feb. 3, 2006) reported on an unusual move from Iran. The global economy is so insecure that something this small could actually start a final domino affect:

> Beginning in 2003, Iran began demanding oil payment in euros, not dollars, although the oil itself was still priced in U.S. currency. Now, Iran is seriously considering establishing an Iranian Oil Bourse, with the goal of competing with the New York Mercantile Exchange, NYMEX, and London's International Petroleum Exchange, IPE.

> Right now, the NYMEX and IPE use three oil "markers" to establish price – West Texas Intermediate crude, Norway Brent crude and the UAE Dubai crude. With the establishment of an Iranian Oil Bourse, Tehran wants to create a fourth oil marker, this one **priced in the euro**.

> Today, about 70 percent of the world's international foreign currency reserves are held in dollars. If the petroeuro begins to challenge the petrodollar, this percentage could diminish drastically.

The United States depends on the dollar foreign-currency reserves in order to sell the Treasury debt that sustains budget deficits. Most Americans are completely unaware of this threat Iran represents to the U.S. economy.

Even China has been hinting at shifting some of its reserves from the dollar to the euro. There is much economic uneasiness in the world today, and this is about to lead into an unprecedented economic upheaval worldwide.

The Fifth Thunder

The next three thunders have a duality that includes both the Church of God and the world. It has already been explained that the Sixth Seal is a time of transition from end-time tribulation on the Church to end-time tribulation on this world. The last three thunders are a direct part of that transition.

#5 The **Fifth Thunder** is **death.**

The first three thunders obviously include a marked increase in death from escalation in worldwide devastation. This thunder is in addition to that destruction and will occur in a specific manner.

All seven thunders should serve to be a very sobering witness (testimony) to the validity that the final end-time destruction, as recorded in prophecy, is now at hand and that God's end-time spokesman for His two witnesses has now come and he is indeed from God. The Seven Thunders will be the beginning evidence that my words are true.

In small part, the Fifth Thunder has already begun within the

Church of God that was scattered. The world will be fully unaware of the first phase of this thunder because they do not know God's Church. However, the Church that was scattered will become fully aware of its reality!

This Fifth Thunder is divided into three specific phases of death. **(1) The first phase** is death within the Church of God that was scattered. It will be specifically about a marked increase in the death of its leadership (the ministry). **(2) The second phase** will be a sudden escalation in the death of notable people in the world. **(3) The third phase** will be a sudden escalation of death in the world from plagues.

(1) This first phase of this Fifth Thunder has already begun in a very small way upon the Church of God that was scattered, after the prophesied apostasy (2 Thes. 2). This phase of the Fifth Thunder is given as a great chastening to those who have been scattered so that they can be shaken from the deep spiritual sleep where they so proudly rest. Sadly, spiritual arrogance and pride are so deeply entrenched in the hearts and minds of those who have been refusing to hear God's warnings, that many will not be able to humble themselves enough to accept what God's end-time prophet is telling them. They will not acknowledge his words, which are from God to them, because they do not like the way they are being addressed. Instead, these will stubbornly cling to their own ideas of how they believe God should teach them through their own organizations.

This phase of the Fifth Thunder is one of **my own choosing**, which God has granted me as part of His own will and purpose for the Church (this will be clarified more fully in the Sixth Thunder). The method of this one last great chastening, that is for the purpose of helping to awaken some from the spiritual coma they are in, is one that God has left for me to determine as one of His end-time witnesses, who will be given far greater power to pronounce plagues "as often as they will" (Revelation 11:6) in order to help humble mankind so they will repent and turn to God.

This specific phase of the Fifth Thunder is given in order to awaken brethren (spiritually) to the last opportunity they will have to repent, in order to enter the promised time they have been taught about ever since their minds were first opened to God's word. All who fail to repent will die in the final tribulation and be awakened to judgment at the end of the 1,000 years of God's reign on earth.

God has already shown the number of those who will respond. It is given in the form of a percentage from the fifth chapter in Ezekiel. At present, only a tithe of the tithe of one-third that was scattered has repented (1% of a third that was scattered). During this first phase, repentance will be offered to another ninety per cent of a full tithe of a third that was scattered (9% of a third that was scattered). This means very little to those of you who are reading this unless you have been part of God's Church. These words are for them and not you. You do not need to understand this, but the Church that was scattered does have the ability to know what is being stated by this prophecy.

God has shown that He has taken His protection away from His ministry that was scattered (those ministers who have not repented). This began to be made manifest less than a year ago. Although it was news in many parts of the world when it happened (I was in Australia and it was in the news there), the world did not take much notice of an event that happened in one of the scattered groups less than a year ago. On March 12, 2005, in a hotel in Wisconsin where some had gathered for Sabbath services, a disgruntled member of their congregation entered the meeting room and fired 22 bullets from a 9mm handgun within a minute, killing seven people. Before the shooting stopped, the pastor, the pastor's son and five other church members were dead and four others were wounded. Then, the disgruntled member killed himself.

This news thundered throughout the scattered Church. Many asked how this could have happened, since nothing like this had ever happened in any Sabbath service meeting in all the history of God's Church. The answer to this is not one that the scattered Church wants to hear—God has removed His protection from all who have refused to repent!

In the same organization, only three months later, one of the three television presenters, a long time pastor of the Church, died from a staph infection. This too rattled this organization and others. This man was beloved and respected by many, including myself. He performed the wedding ceremony for my wife and me. A few years later, he was among the ministers who laid hands upon me when I was ordained into the ministry of God's Church.

In addition to this minister's death, the very minister that assisted him died from the same kind of staph infection only two months later.

These three ministers, who died within the past year, were part of the same organization, the Living Church of God. The significance of the death of two of its ministers from an infectious disease should not go unnoticed in the environs of the scattered Church because the prayers of the congregation for the healing of both ministers went unanswered.

This is important to understand because the leader of this group, Mr. Roderick Meredith, has requested that all people in his organization fast before God, asking Him for the gift of healing upon their ministers for the purpose of helping people in the world see that they are the organization that God is working through to do His Work on earth. Mr. Meredith has asked this of his membership on several different occasions over the past few years. God has not heard their prayers or accepted these fasts!

Not only has God not granted their petitions, but the very thing that Mr. Meredith requested is against God's will for this end-time. Not only was it wrong to request his organization to fast in this way, but the method for revealing through whom God is working will not be done through the manifestation of miraculous healings performed by ministers. God did use this as part of a means to reveal the glory of His Son, Jesus Christ, and He did grant this power in a great way to the early Church as a powerful witness of His new Church and who His ministers were.

However, for this end-time, it is not God's purpose to display signs of miraculous healings to the world in order to show where He is working. It is His purpose to bring an end to man's self-rule by humbling man so that he will repent and turn to Him and receive His government, once Jesus Christ returns as King of kings. The last era of God's Church must be humbled so that it will repent and return to Him, and this world must also be humbled in order to receive Him. God will humble the Church, and He will humble the world through end-time events described throughout this book. It is by this very means that God will reveal through whom He is now working. Specifically regarding His two end-time witnesses, it will be by the power given to them for destruction and plagues, not healing! Yes, this is the means that will help humble those who will yet be awakened to repentance in the environs of the scattered Church. Escalating deaths in the leadership of the scattered groups will serve as a witness of who it is through whom God is working. It will *not* be done through miraculous signs of healing.

As in the story of Elijah and the ministers of Baal, the words of Elijah were upheld with great power, and God revealed through whom He was working. The same will be true in the things that will happen to members of the leadership of the scattered Church who refuse to repent and hear God's true servant.

The deaths of these three ministers, from the Living Church of God, will now begin to take on greater symbolic meaning for everyone in the scattered Church of God groups. God's protection has been removed from the scattered Church, as well as His intervention in healing; because people have not repented of the reasons the Church was scattered in the first place. So now, death will begin to spread throughout the scattered Church, and most noticeably among the leadership.

Elijah's Story Repeated

There is a story in the Book of Kings that is about to be repeated on a spiritual plane for God's Church. Israel became separated from God and turned to other ideas about God. They turned to Baal worship by mingling the teachings of Baal with those of God.

Elijah challenged all the prophets of Baal and told the Israelites that they should quit stumbling back and forth between two different thoughts about God:

> *And Elijah came to all the people, and said, "How long will you falter between two opinions? If the ETERNAL is God, follow Him, but if Baal is then follow him." But the people couldn't answer him a word.* (1 Kings 18:21).

Elijah was only one man, so what he said about God was

difficult for people to accept. They chose to be more comfortable by supporting the soothing teachings of the prophets of Baal. Elijah then challenged the prophets of Baal to show that either they were right about God or that he was right about God.

Elijah had those prophets prepare a sacrifice for an offering to Baal. If Baal was God, then he should be able to consume this offering in the sight of the people. These prophets cried to Baal all morning long. Elijah mocked them because their prayers were not being answered. Elijah then goaded them by saying that they should cry out louder because perhaps Baal could not hear them or perhaps he was talking to others. Perhaps Baal was on a journey or sleeping and needed to be awakened; or maybe he was away someplace relieving himself (an expression used for going to the toilet).

Finally, by the time for the evening sacrifice, Elijah prepared an offering on an altar of wood. Water was poured over the sacrifice three different times and a trench that surrounded the altar was filled with water:

> *And the water ran around the altar, and he also filled the trench with water. And it came to pass at the time for the offering of the evening sacrifice, that Elijah the prophet came near, and said, "ETERNAL God of Abraham, Isaac, and of Israel, let it be known this day that you are God in Israel, and that I am your servant, and that I have done all these things by your word. Hear me, O ETERNAL, hear me, that this people may know that you are the ETERNAL God, and that you have turned their heart back again." Then the fire of the ETERNAL fell, and consumed the burnt sacrifice, and the wood, and the stones, and the dust, and licked up the water that was in the trench. And when all the people saw it, they fell on their faces, and they said,*

*"The ETERNAL, he is the God; the ETERNAL, he is the
God." Then Elijah said to them, "Take the prophets of
Baal; let not one of them escape." So they took them and
Elijah brought them down to the brook Kishon, and killed
them there.* (1 Kings 18:35-40)

It is time for the spiritual application of this story of Elijah to
be fulfilled. Four hundred and fifty prophets of Baal died that
day. Now, the time has come for a type of this same account to
be fulfilled in the environs of the spiritual Israel of God, the
Church of God.

I have also made a petition to the ETERNAL God of Abraham.
My petition is that this first phase of the Fifth Thunder be
fulfilled exactly as it is written here. This request is so that
scattered brethren who are asleep might be awakened and know
that God has granted them the opportunity to repent and return to
Him at this time. Also, it is so that they may know that I am His
end-time prophet, His spokesman for the two end-time witnesses.

It will be revealed in a very short time whether I am God's
prophet or not, as well as whether scattered Church leaders are
God's ministers any longer or not. As stated in a previous
chapter, either one of these is true or neither is true.

To make it absolutely clear, my petition covers more in regard
to the scattered ministers. The most notable among them will be
those who die toward the beginning. However, **every** minister
who was scattered, who fails to repent early on and return to God
(with me, as God's minister, teaching them) will die during the
final three and one-half years of great tribulation. They will not
be in the first resurrection, and they will not see the millennial
reign of God's Kingdom on earth.

The most notable deaths early on, which are yet to come to
pass, will be the two remaining television presenters in the Living

Church of God. The sound of this thunder will be intensified by the early deaths of the leaders of the Philadelphia Church of God, the Restored Church of God and the Church of the Great God. Then, those in the largest scattered group, who think they have escaped, will be lifted up to believe that God is with them because they are so filled with pride. But, when that happens, the deaths of many in the United Church of God will begin.

How much more specific can one be to show that he is either of God, and indeed His prophet, or someone who has clearly stepped over the line to be dealt with by God in a speedy manner. Time will tell! And, you don't have long to wait!

(2) The second phase of death will be upon notable people in the world. It will begin small and increase in intensity as all the thunders do. These notable people will include political leaders and well known entertainment and sports figures. It will include other religious figures within the various religions of the world. The primary exception to this will be the Pope of the Catholic Church, who is prophesied to die directly after the return of Jesus Christ. This phase will overlap the first, but this is the main one that people in the world will notice.

(3) The third phase of death will come from epidemics and pandemics in the world. Over this past year, many governments in the world have started minimal preparations for a possible pandemic from bird flu. This and much more are coming upon the world scene. As God has warned throughout time, the end-time will be the worst time in man's history.

The Sixth Thunder
This thunder also concerns both the Church and the world. It

started very small with the publication of my first book, *The Prophesied End-Time*. The content of that book is strong concerning the announcement of prophesied end-time events that have already begun, but the pronouncement that I am an end-time prophet is a declaration that will have profound significance for God's Church.

The growing manifestation of proof that I am God's end-time prophet and that I am the spokesman of His two end-time witnesses is a thunder that will become powerfully stronger all the way up until the very return of Jesus Christ.

#6   The **Sixth Thunder** is the growing **revelation of God's end-time witnesses**. That revelation is that I am the spokesman of God's two end-time prophets—the spokesman of His two end-time witnesses.

This thunder will grow louder as the events described in the previous thunders continue to unfold with ever increasing intensity, proving the validity of what has been written and that what I am saying is true. Radio and television interviews will become more the norm as curiosity, news, controversy, and fear increase in proportion to the growing intensity of these thunders.

A few quotes need to be repeated here. They are recorded earlier in this chapter, and they have everything to do with this Sixth Thunder:

> The Seven Thunders will be declared in the
> remainder of this chapter. Those thunders have never
> been announced before now. Everything else that John
> wrote, concerning the Seven Seals, Seven Trumpets and
> the Seven Last Plagues, was each declared by an angel.

The Seven Thunders did not come from angels. John heard the sound of Seven Thunders. This was a message about an end-time prophet of God. The specifics of the Seven Thunders were left for this end-time in order to be declared—to be pronounced—by God's end-time prophet, the spokesperson of the two end-time witnesses. More about this will be explained in the Sixth Thunder.

The Seven Thunders have much to do with **how** God will reveal His two witnesses. These thunders serve as a prelude to the final tribulation and the greater manifestation of those two witnesses.

The revelation of the Seven Thunders has everything to do with the revelation of God's end-time witness *about* man and God's revelation of His two witnesses *to* man! Sadly, most will **choose** to ignore what they hear.

God did not allow the apostle John to write about the Seven Thunders. John did not hear what each specific thunder was, but he heard part of what was said about how the thunders would be revealed. John was an apostle and a prophet, in that he recorded all that God inspired him to write. He wrote the Book of Revelation, but it was not given to him to understand all that he had written. As John's counterpart, God has given me the understanding of the revelations given to John. In addition, I am the spokesman, one of the very end-time prophets and witnesses that John wrote about.

In interviews that followed the publication of my first book and in correspondence sent to me since then, the question was often asked, "How did God reveal these things to you?" It is by the same means that God has so often used in the past to reveal His will and purpose to His servants, the prophets of old. God does this through inspiration of His spirit, the conveying of His very thoughts (words) to the mind (thoughts) of those with whom He is working. Many throughout the ages, and even now, falsely make this claim as the means that God has spoken to them. False religious teachers have made a mockery of this means that God has used to reveal His true will to His people.

The question about how God has revealed His truth to me is a fair one. The answer that I am who I say I am will be given by the events described in both books coming true exactly as I have described. This will be the proof that I am God's end-time witness and spokesman. But **before** great power is given to me to perform miraculous events similar to those of Moses (but with far greater power), once the Seventh Seal is opened and the final three and one-half years of worldwide tribulation begins, God has reserved these Seven Thunders for me to declare.

These Seven Thunders are a **combination** of God's inspiration in me to know His purpose and being at one with Him concerning His will for this end-time. These thunders are largely a matter of my own choosing, which God has given to me since I am His spokesman and the one who will stand before Him to the whole world during this end-time (Revelation 11:4 & Zechariah 4:14).

All Seven Thunders are given as God's proof that I am His end-time prophet.

God has given me the job of declaring His witness *of* man *to* man, as part of bringing an end to man's self rule and the establishing of His Kingdom, His government on earth.

The Seventh Thunder

The revelation of this last thunder will be covered in far greater depth in the last chapter. This last thunder, as with the previous two thunders, concerns the Church and the world.

#7   The Seventh Thunder is the accelerated revelation of God to man.

This book has explained how man has never really known God and that there is great confusion and contradiction in religious beliefs concerning Him. It has also been shown that through the entire time of man on earth that only a little more than 144,000 people have truly known God.

God has not revealed Himself to most of mankind. Only a few throughout the past six millennia have been able to come to know God. Those few, who did come to know God, were rejected by the rest of mankind. The prophets and apostles were rejected by man, therefore, man was not able to know God. Yet, even these servants of God did not address the entirety of mankind. God taught His ways to only one nation in Moses' time, but most of that nation rejected His words.

The history of man (the true witness of man) is that man does not want God's ways. Man has not wanted God to govern his life. So, in the past 6,000 years, God has called a very few into a special relationship with Him in order to be taught and trained for a future world ruling government—the Kingdom of God that will be established over all the earth at the return of Jesus Christ.

Much of this has already been explained, but it needs to be understood that God is getting ready to do what He has never done before with mankind. God is getting ready to reveal Himself to the entirety of mankind. This revelation is similar to thunder.

It has already begun to sound within His Church. It is about to sound powerfully throughout the world as His two witnesses grow in power, as all of God's prophesied end-time events begin to unfold in an ever increasing manner. As this process progresses, God will continue to reveal Himself more fully.

God's revelation to mankind will continue to accelerate as we draw closer to the end of man's rulership and the coming of Jesus Christ to rule over all the earth. Man has not known God, but all this is beginning to change. It has begun first and foremost within His Church. His revelation will continue in greater power and might as we draw closer to the time His Son returns to rule.

The Church of God, over the past twenty years, has prided itself in the knowledge of God. This pride, with its presumptuous attitude, is the reason the Church was scattered. Of all people, one would think that God's own Church would know Him fully; but they have not. Over the last hundred years and before, God did not give His people all knowledge about Himself and His Son. Part of that knowledge was withheld from God's end-time apostle, Mr. Herbert W. Armstrong. This knowledge was reserved so that it could be revealed at the time that God revealed His end-time spokesman, as a proof of His seal on His two end-time witnesses.

Much of the Church will reject this revelation about God just as they will reject the identity of His two witnesses. Some are already mocking this knowledge. However, some will begin to repent and turn to God again once they see the Seven Thunders coming true. They will be awakened from a spiritual sleep.

At first, this thunder is for God's own Church. Then, as we enter the time of the Seventh Seal, this knowledge will begin to spread throughout the world until the day that everyone will be able to know God.

Chapter 5

THE FINAL THREE
& ONE-HALF YEARS

This chapter will address the sequence of events which will unfold during the final three and one-half years of man's self-rule on earth. These events are not pleasant to read about because they are catastrophic beyond belief. These events will begin when the Seventh Seal is opened.

We have arrived at one of the most fearful moments in time that is spoken about in the Word of God. It is a time like no other. God said that there has never been a time like this, nor ever will be again. It is a time that will teach some of the greatest lessons of life to all mankind. God has determined that the lessons from this time are to be indelibly etched into the minds of all who have ever lived.

The magnitude of this end-time destruction is very unpleasant to contemplate. It is difficult to write about, and it will be difficult to read. However, you need to see this time for what it is, as unpleasant as it is; then you can better understand the deeper reasons "why" such things are going to be allowed by God, which is the subject of the following chapter.

The next chapter will explain **"why"** this end-time of worldwide destruction has to occur the way in which God has revealed.

Opening the Seventh Seal

When Jesus Christ opens the Seventh Seal of Revelation, God declares that the final three and one-half years of great tribulation will begin, and man's self-rule will be brought to an end. Satan's influence and power over man will also be brought to an end at this time. He will not be allowed to have any influence over man for nearly 1,000 years, after which time, he will be allowed to do so once again for one final, very short period of time.

Once the Seventh Seal is opened, the first of Seven Trumpets will be blown. Each Trumpet will announce a specific phase of great tribulation on the earth. The first four trumpets will proclaim the demise of the United States and her closest allies. All of this will be explained in this chapter.

The final sequence of events that leads up to the opening of the Seventh Seal needs to be briefly reviewed. By the time this final seal is opened, all 144,000 whom God has called over six millennia will be fully trained to rule in His Kingdom. This Kingdom will be established when Jesus Christ returns with the 144,000 on the last day of the final three and one-half years of man's self-rule. The remaining few, who were yet to be added to this total count of 144,000, and are alive at this end-time, will be sealed (completed their training) by the time this last seal is opened. This final sealing will occur during the time of the Sixth Seal.

During the Sixth Seal, all Seven Thunders will be getting progressively louder. Before the Seventh (and final) Seal is opened, the Seven Thunders will become so pronounced that the validity of everything written about them in the previous chapter should roar loudly in the ears of anyone who is willing to admit the truth. But even then, many still will prefer to believe a lie! They still will prefer to be falsely soothed by denying reality and the truth.

Also, by this moment in time, there will be a strong, rapidly growing recognition within the United States that I am who I say I am—one of God's end-time witnesses and His prophet. This Sixth Thunder will continue to grow much louder through this final three and one-half years.

The First Four Trumpets

The first four trumpet blasts will announce four powerfully destructive events that will bring about **the total collapse of the United States**, the United Kingdom, Canada, Australia, New Zealand, and some countries of Western Europe. The direct effect of all four events is first and foremost upon the United States.

The events, declared by these first four trumpets, are a prophetic fulfillment of the symbolism contained in the events of 9-11, when the World Trade Towers and the Pentagon were struck by terrorism. It is during the time of the first four trumpets when the symbolism of 9-11 is accomplished; the economy, government and military might of the greatest nation on earth is struck a fatal blow.

The chain reaction, which will follow, is the very thing that will lead immediately into World War III. It will be the last war that mankind will ever fight! Before this final three and one-half years comes to a complete end, all military forces around the world will have been destroyed, every economy will be decimated, several billion people will have died, and vast destruction will cover every part of the earth.

The First Trumpet

The First Trumpet blast will occur quickly after the Seventh Seal of Revelation is opened by Jesus Christ. Even as I am writing, the events prophesied to take place during these trumpet blasts are already showing signs of emerging on the world scene. Much of what will occur is simply being held back by God until it is His time to allow it. God is going to allow mankind to bring about one more world war. If God were not in control of the timing, some of these events would have already begun; but God is in control of the exact timing of everything that is to take place. God will cut the end-time short by allowing these end-time events to occur over the limited space of three and one-half years, otherwise, mankind would end up destroying all life on the earth—so says God Almighty! Notice the powerful description of the first trumpet:

> *When He* [Jesus Christ] *had opened the seventh seal, there was silence in heaven for about the space of half an hour. And I saw seven angels who stood before God, and seven trumpets were given to them. And another angel who had a golden censer came and stood at the altar, and he was given much incense that he should offer it with the prayers of all saints upon the golden altar which was before the throne. Then the smoke of the incense along with the prayers of the saints ascended up before God out of the angel's hand. And the angel took the censer, and filled it with fire from the altar, and cast it to the earth. Then there were voices, and thundering, and lightning, and an earthquake. And the seven angels who had the seven trumpets prepared themselves to sound. After the first angel sounded, then there followed hail and fire mingled with blood, and they were cast on the earth, and the third part of trees were burned up and the green grass with it was burned up.* (Revelation 8:1-7)

This first powerful event of the Seventh Seal will result in wide-spread destruction over the United States and beyond her border into Canada. The destruction in Canada will be less, but she will experience repercussions from what will happen in the U.S.; because she is a neighbor, as well as a prophetic brother. When we are told that a third of all plant life will be destroyed, that is exactly what it means. The actual event will not be disclosed until it is time for it to happen. As with all the Seals of Revelation, many of the specifics of each of the Seven Trumpets will not be revealed until it is time for the actual events to take place. It should also be noted, that in the first trumpet there is fire mingled with blood. Blood means there will be much death when this event occurs. Most of it will be the death of animals and birds, but also a large number of people will die—into the tens of thousands.

The Second Trumpet

> *Then the second angel sounded and there was something like a great mountain burning with fire that was cast into the sea, and a third part of the sea became like blood. And a third part of the living creatures which were in the sea died, and a third part of the ships were destroyed.* (Revelation 8:8-9)

This event will take place primarily over water, but its effect will also decimate much of the coastline of the United States, the United Kingdom and some of their allies, including the complete destruction of some cities. A third of all the waters within the boundaries of these countries will become lifeless; everything will die in these areas. This death will include a third of all the people on boats and ships. However, there will be hundreds of thousands who will die on the coastal areas of these same regions.

The reason for the destruction of so many shipping vessels is that this event occurs primarily in port cities where there are large concentrations of ships, commerce and people.

The Third Trumpet

Then the third angel sounded and what appeared like a great star fell from heaven, burning like a torch, and it fell on a third part of the rivers and on the springs of waters. The name of the star is called Wormwood, and a third of the waters became wormwood, and many men died from the waters because they were made bitter. (Revelation 8:10-11).

Each of these three events will become progressively more devastating upon the United States and her closest allies. This lethal blow will finally cripple the most prosperous and powerful nation the world has ever known. The initial destruction from this event will include several large cities. It will make the devastation from Hurricane Katrina appear **extremely small** by comparison. The destruction of property will be beyond measure, but the destruction of life will be far greater. The death toll will be in the tens of millions.

Worldwide repercussions from this event will trigger World War III.

The Fourth Trumpet

Then the fourth angel sounded, and a third of the sun was struck, and a third of the moon, and a third of the stars, so that a third of them were darkened. So the sun did not shine for a third of the day, and likewise the night. Then I looked, and I heard an angel flying through the midst of heaven, saying with a loud voice, "Woe, woe, woe, to the inhabitants of the earth because of the trumpet blasts from the three angels who are yet to sound!" (Revelation 8:12-13)

The cumulative effect from the first three trumpet blasts will be announced by this fourth blast, which will cause much more destruction. By this time, over one-third of the population of the United States, the United Kingdom and their closest allies will have died. Many more will continue to die from the results of this fourth event. Weather conditions will be horribly altered on earth as a result of one-third of the sun's light no longer being able to warm the earth and give light. Plant life and normal growing cycles will not be sustained by the sun as in the past. This will result in immediate famine over many areas of the earth. The effects from the Fourth Trumpet blast will result in far greater death—again—tens of millions.

Although the devastation that follows the first four trumpet blasts result in unimaginable destruction, along with the death of a few hundred million people, the last verse of Revelation 8 gives a warning of far worse events that will follow.

After the announcements sounded from the first four trumpets, a greater warning is given:

Then I looked, and I heard an angel flying through the midst of heaven, saying with a loud voice, "Woe, woe, woe, to the inhabitants of the earth because of the trumpet blasts from the three angels who are yet to sound!" (Revelation 8:13).

The expression "woe" refers to dire consequences that will be far more destructive in the world. There are three "woes," which refer to the events that will follow in the last three trumpet blasts.

The downfall of the United States and her closest allies will lead to a great power vacuum in the world; nations will race to fill the void. Many areas of the world, that have been held at bay by the influence of the United States and her closest allies, will now be determined to accomplish their will on others. Just consider the nations that have had long lasting border and territorial disputes, as well as religious and political disputes which have been contained. Now they are held back no longer!

The Fifth Trumpet

The blast from the Fifth Trumpet will announce the emergence of a great political power and a great religious power on earth. The Biblical symbolisms contained in the description of the message from this trumpet blast are prophetically unique. Rather than having readers become bogged down with an overwhelming amount of Biblical study that serves no purpose here, I will simply give an overview of the meaning and outcome.

This trumpet will announce the first great "woe" on the earth. The prophetic description covers many overlapping, unfolding and interacting highlighted events in the final three and one-half years of man's self-rule. The highlights of this Fifth Trumpet include:

(1) the emergence of Satan and his large army of demons to great power

(2) the emergence of great power wielded by the Roman Catholic Church and the Pope

(3) the emergence of a fully-united European union of ten nations

(4) the emergence of a colossal military might from this united European union and the destruction of several hundred million people by it

(5) the protection of God's elect and the torment and trying (testing) of those who have refused to repent in the environs of God's scattered Church

All these events begin once the fifth trumpet is sounded:

Then the fifth angel sounded, and I saw a star fall from heaven to the earth, and to him was given the key of the bottomless pit. And he opened the bottomless pit, and there arose smoke out of the pit like the smoke from a great furnace, and the sun and the air were darkened because of the smoke of the pit. Out of the smoke there came locusts upon the earth, and they were given power like scorpions of the earth have power. (Revelation 9:1-3)

Satan's Rise to Power

In prophecy, stars are symbolic of angels. One simple example of a star that is misinterpreted by the world of traditional Christianity is the one that led the wise men to Bethlehem, where the Messiah was born. Traditional Christianity pictures this as a literal star over the little town of Bethlehem. Yet, most people do not know that it wasn't a literal star in the heavens, but an angel that directed them where to go.

The star in Revelation 9:1 refers to Satan. John's vision represents Satan's fall from God's presence to his banishment here on earth. Satan, and those angels who rebelled with him against God, have been limited in the power they once were given. They have been restrained by God. This restraint from power is symbolically pictured by chains and a place of restraint, like a prison. The key is symbolic of being released from these restraints.

Satan has been allowed to exercise powers of influence over mankind, primarily in the form of feeding man's own greed for wealth, power, illegal self-gratification, etc. Now, at this very point of end-time tribulation, at the sounding of the Fifth Trumpet, Satan and the demons (angels that rebelled with Satan) will be released from their restraints and will be able to exercise far greater power and influence over mankind than before. Nations and religions already desire to exert power and evil on earth, but Satan will move them to follow their evil desires more quickly.

In actuality, God will be accelerating a natural course of events that would otherwise be spread over many more years of intense suffering, war, and evil on earth, which would result in far greater destruction. If God did not speed up these events, as revealed through the Seven Trumpets, and limit this time to only three and one-half years, then all life would be erased from off the earth.

The Final Rise of a United Europe

For over fifty years now, Europe has been moving toward a union of nations. It began in the early 1950's with the vision of a stronger European economy being formed through the European Common Market. This finally evolved into a greater unification through the governing power of the European Union. There has been a constant driving force within Europe to unite under a stronger governing organization of nations. Over time, a core block of those nations forged a stronger bond by the adoption of a common currency—the euro. Political and even military consolidation has continued to press forward.

For over fifty years, God's Church has foretold the rise of this united Europe, which would have a common currency, a military and religion (Roman Catholic Church), and would finally consist of only ten united countries.

For many years now, there has been a growing desire among many Europeans for the revival of an old Europe into a single United States of Europe, replacing and surpassing the United

States of America as the predominant power in the world. Many in Europe are frustrated with, what they see, as too slow a pace in the progress of these goals. A bond of unity among some of these nations is becoming stronger, while their frustrations are mounting against those who are seen as slowing the process. There is deep resentment and growing bitterness toward these nations (especially Great Britain) who won't join together for a stronger euro.

Although many other areas of prophecy can help you understand what will happen at the time of this Fifth Trumpet, only the conclusions from the revelation of those prophecies will be covered in this chapter. More of this information is covered in *The Prophesied End-Time.*

Satan's release from restraint will move him to exercise greater power and influence over the unity of Europe. Satan has exercised his influence and power to deceive and create havoc during every revival of the Holy Roman Empire. He will stir up ten nations in Europe who will take control of all power over the European Union. Only those ten nations will agree to lend their power *as one*.

Germany will once again be the principal driving force behind a united Europe. As in the sixth revival of the Holy Roman Empire, which led into World War II, this seventh prophetic and last revival will lead into a full blown World War III. And, like a scorpion that strikes quickly without notice, a new United States of Europe will swiftly exercise great military power that it already has in its possession under the **cloak** of NATO. This will occur at a very specific moment in time. This new European power, which would eventually move to accomplish the same thing, will move forward more quickly due to the influence of Satan and his army of demons.

The account of this next revelation will infuriate many people, nevertheless, it is true. At the same time that Satan will have powerful influence over ten nations in Europe, he will wield great deceptive power over the Roman Catholic Church. For centuries, the Catholic Church has been led into deception through Satan's power; but he will exercise even greater direct control at this final end-time. Although there will be a distorted bond between this new Europe and the Catholic Church, that bond will become deeply stressed as these two struggle for dominant power, one against the other.

Indeed, God will make it clear who is the true power over both the revived Europe and the Catholic Church—it is Satan:

And they had a king over them who is the angel of the bottomless pit, whose name in the Hebrew tongue is Abaddon [destruction]*, but in the Greek tongue he has the name Apollyon* [destroyer]*. (Revelation 9:11)

God's Church

At the same time all these events come together at the sounding of the Fifth Trumpet, there will be an initial period of time (five months) when much human suffering will continue as a result of the first four trumpets. This marks a time of great suffering on a worldwide scale, but even now, God's Church is still part of these prophetic events. God's Church still exists on earth, and will continue, all the way up to the very return of Jesus Christ; but many who were scattered in the Church, after the great falling away, will not live into the new millennial period that follows.

Although Satan and his demons will be released from great restraint, they will still be restrained in their ability to cause hurt to any of God's people who obey Him, especially those who are sealed as part of the 144,000. It will be during this time that Satan and his followers will be allowed to wreak havoc and torment upon those who have not yet repented and humbly turned to God's end-time prophets for understanding.

Those of the scattered Church of God, who are tormented during this five-month period, will suffer greatly for their stubborn pride and continued defiance against God. Once this time has ended as a final time of trying, all of those who have resisted God through selfish pride will die and will not be allowed to enter the millennial period that will soon follow. Instead, they will be awakened (from death) at the end of this time in the great resurrection. There will be much weeping and gnashing of teeth. At this time they will finally see the foolishness of their choices, and they will also see what they gave up.

This five-month period will also be paralleled by millions of people who will begin to repent and seek God. They will begin to turn to the truth they have heard from God's end-time prophets, as well as those who serve with them in God's Church. Yet, during this same time, those who still refuse to repent (in the United States, Canada, Australia, New Zealand, and some western European countries) will experience great trial and torment to help them see their stubborn pride and bring them to repentance.

Much Revelation Yet Reserved

Nothing more specific on the Fifth Trumpet can be given at this time. A little more is mentioned in my first book, but not much. It is God's purpose that many of the details of these events, and the revelation of their complete meaning, be reserved for another time. This time will be just prior to their actual occurrence or at the moment they begin to take place on earth. This will be reserved for greater revelation from God's two end-time witnesses at this very time.

The same is true about much of what is being covered in this chapter about the Seven Trumpets. It is not yet God's purpose that all these things be revealed.

During the time covered in the Fifth Trumpet, several hundred million people will die—more than the total number who died during the period of the first four trumpets. Finally, this time will also come to an end, as John wrote, *"One woe is past, and behold, there are two more woes coming after this"* (Rev. 9:12).

The Sixth Trumpet

Although Europe will step in to fill the power vacuum left by the collapse of the United States, there will be other countries that will immediately begin to prepare for world conquest. They know Europe, and they will not have Europe exercise control over their future:

> *Then the sixth angel sounded, and I heard a voice from the four horns of the golden altar, which is before God, saying to the sixth angel who had the trumpet, "Release the four angels which are bound in the great river Euphrates." The four angels were released, who had been prepared for the hour, and day, and month, and year, to kill a third of mankind. The number of the army of the horsemen was two hundred million, and I heard the number of them.* (Revelation 9:13-16)

China and other countries of Asia will form an alliance that will create an army which will exceed two hundred million. They will have fearsome power to destroy everything in their path, and this is what they will set out to do. They will seek control—total control of the earth.

Little needs to be said about this here. However, you need to know that this great "woe" upon mankind will result in one-third of all mankind being destroyed, as it will account for the death of well over **2 billion** people. This will indeed be a great woe on earth!

Pride runs deep in human nature. Mankind will continue to resist God, even after all the horrifying events of the previous six trumpets have occurred. By the end of the period covering the first six trumpets, several billion people will have died. Multiple millions around the world, who have been conquered by these two great powers, will have come to repentance. Yet, there are many who will refuse to repent, including the vast populations of these two great superpowers. They will insist on living life as they please. This is what is being spoken of in the verses which follow the description of the army that numbers two hundred million:

> *But the rest of mankind, who were not killed by these plagues, still would not repent of the works of their hands, that they should not worship demons, and idols of gold, and silver, and brass, and stone, and of wood, which neither can see, nor hear, nor walk. Neither would they repent of their murders, nor of their sorceries, nor of their fornication, nor of their thefts.* (Revelation 9:20-21)

By this point in time, many will have repented. They will have been humbled because they will have been conquered. Those still ruling will continue to live as they please, and they will have no intention of repenting and turning to God. This is a witness of the haughty spirit in mankind. Unless humbled, man will not listen to God. So, that is exactly what God will do—He will humble both superpowers.

Armageddon

The last great battle of mankind (described in Revelation and prophetically known as Armageddon) is the account of these two superpowers converging upon one another and the battle that ensues. This confrontation is inevitable. This time coincides with the very end of the three and one-half years of final end-time tribulation.

The actual region of Megiddo is known anciently in Biblical times as the place of several great military slaughters. Therefore, the name has great significance in prophetic symbolism in relation to this final confrontation of mankind and the end of man's rule on earth.

China and her allies will move against the United States of Europe. These superpowers will pursue a head-on confrontation of military might, since both will be reluctant to use any more nuclear weapons because of the enormous destruction already experienced. However, it should be noted that if either began to lose the battle, such weapons would be used, and this nuclear confrontation would indeed end in the total annihilation of all life on the earth. God will not allow this to happen. This is why supernatural intervention in the timing of events is so critical.

Therefore, on this last day of the three and one-half years of great tribulation, God will intervene in the affairs of all mankind, thus, saving mankind from destroying himself. This day is called the day of God's great wrath. It will be the last day of man's self-rule over the past six millennia.

Man's awesome technological developments over the past century have been withheld from mankind for great reason. Man would not have lasted for six millennia if God had allowed such development before now. This is the precise reason God created a language barrier at the tower of Babel, scattering man over the earth (Genesis 11). A few thousand years ago, God actually caused different groups of people to begin speaking in different languages in order to withhold such technological advances.

God knew what the growth of technology would bring. He also knew that nations would use it for personal power, military advantage, and finally, war. Such is the nature of man. The arms race has been just that—a race for the most powerful, the most advanced and the most destructive weapons. The true witness of man is that he will always use such weapons on one another, as a result of man's thirst for power and dominance.

Yes, if God did not intervene, mankind would destroy all life on earth. This is why God will cut short man's time by the rapid development of end-time events which will be completed over three and one-half years. God will do this in order to minimize an otherwise prolonged and hideous suffering on earth.

Man's Last Day

This last day of man's self-rule will be the greatest single day of destruction in all history, but it will also bring the greatest "good news" to man that anyone could ever hope to imagine.

The day the Seventh Trumpet is blown will be the third and final "woe" upon the earth. But three and one-half days prior to this, God's two witnesses will be killed in the streets of Jerusalem. This event will lead to the first great event that will begin on that last day:

> *And when they* [the two witnesses] *shall have finished their testimony, the beast that ascends out of the bottomless pit* [Satan through his influence on men] *shall make war against them, and shall overcome them, and kill them. And their dead bodies shall lie in the street of*

the great city [in Jerusalem], *which spiritually is called Sodom and Egypt, where also our Lord* [Jesus Christ] *was crucified. And they of the people and kindreds and tongues and nations shall see their dead bodies three and one-half days* [via modern technology], *and their dead bodies shall not be allowed to be put in graves. And those who dwell on the earth* [of the two superpowers] *will rejoice over them, being delighted, and shall send gifts to one another because these two prophets tormented them who dwell on the earth.* (Revelation 11:7-10)

God's two witnesses will be viewed by others (who will hate their message about God) as being responsible for their suffering. The two witnesses will be bringing plagues upon the nations of these two superpowers in order to humble them, but they will not be humbled. Instead, these superpowers will continue in their own selfish pride. Satan will have been restrained from causing God's two witnesses any harm until it is God's time to allow them to be killed, but then:

After three and one-half days the Spirit of life from God entered into them [the two witnesses] *and they stood upon their feet. Then great fear fell upon them which saw them. And they heard a great voice from heaven saying unto them, "Come up here." And they ascended up to heaven in a cloud and their enemies saw this happening to them.* (Revelation 11:11-12)

In the actual order of events for this last day, this will be the first event. The day will begin by the appearance, in the highest atmosphere of the earth, of a large area of dazzling light and a powerfully colorful display, which man has never witnessed before. It will be the physical appearance (manifestation) of the coming of Jesus Christ and the resurrection that will take place at this very time. All 144,000 people who have been trained throughout six millennia to be in God's government (the first phase of the Kingdom of God) will be resurrected at the beginning of this day.

It will be at the time of the resurrection of these two witnesses (viewed by millions) that the 144,000 will be resurrected and given eternal life in spirit bodies. The glory of this event will be seen literally from earth. It will be an awesome, yet fearful sight for many on earth. After the resurrection of God's two witnesses we read:

> *In that same hour there was a great earthquake* [in Jerusalem], *and the tenth part of the city fell, and in the earthquake there were seven thousand men killed, and those remaining were made frightened, and they gave glory to the God of heaven.* (Revelation 11:13)

The Seventh Trumpet

In the first great event on the last day of the end-time tribulation, Jesus Christ will be in the heavens above the earth with the 144,000 who will be resurrected. The display from earth will perplex mankind. Some will know the significance and will anticipate Jesus Christ coming, while others, who still resist, will see this awesome display as a threat to their power and existence. Finally, man's reign will be brought to an end:

> *The second woe is past, and behold, the third woe is coming quickly. Then the seventh angel sounded, and there were great voices in heaven, saying, "The kingdoms of this world have now become the kingdoms of our Lord, even of His Christ, and He shall reign from now and forever more"* (Revelation 11:14-15)

This is the announcement that man's reign over the past 6,000 years has finally been brought to an end, and now, God will reign on earth in His Kingdom with Jesus Christ at its head; Christ has now become King of kings over all the earth:

> *Then the twenty four elders, who sat before God on their thrones, fell on their faces and worshipped God, saying, "We give you thanks, O Lord God Almighty, who is, and was, and are yet to come, because you have taken to yourself your great power, and will now reign."* (Rev. 11:16-17)

God has always been in control of His creation, but He chose to allow man to rule himself for 6,000 years. This has always been part of God's plan in order for man to learn that only God's way of life produces good and lasting results. The witness of man's ways over the past 6,000 years has proven to be disastrous.

When the Seventh Trumpet sounds, the time will have come for God to begin His rule over the earth. This has been His plan since before the creation of the universe millions of years ago. As it says in verse 18, the time has come for God to *"destroy them who destroy the earth."*

Seven Last Plagues

The third and final woe that will follow the blast of the Seventh Trumpet is divided into seven specific events, which are called the Seven Last Plagues of God's wrath. This wrath will be on those who still will refuse to submit to God. This wrath will crush the superpowers of Europe and China along with her allies:

> *Then I saw another sign in heaven that was massively great and amazing, with seven angels having the seven last plagues, for in them is filled up the wrath of God . . . Then one of the four creatures gave to the seven angels*

seven golden vials full of the wrath of God, who lives for ever and ever. And the temple was filled with smoke from the glory of God, and from his power, and no one was able to enter into the temple until the seven plagues from the seven angels were fulfilled . . . Then I heard a great voice from the temple saying to the seven angels, "Go your ways, and pour out the vials of the wrath of God upon the earth." The first went and poured out his vial on the earth, and there fell a destroying and disease filled sore upon the men who had the mark of the beast, and upon those who worshipped his image. (Revelation 15:1, 7-8, 16:1-2)

This specific plague of death will fall upon those in the United States of Europe who embrace the teachings of the Catholic Church. This will not be a small thing which God does. It will be powerfully destructive with several hundred thousand dying this day from this First Plague, and the second follows quickly:

And the second angel poured out his vial upon the sea, and it became as the blood of a dead man, and everything living died in the sea. (Verse 3)

Everything in the coastal waters of both superpowers will die, including mankind. At this moment, tens of thousands will die and this death will continue:

The third angel poured out his vial upon the rivers and sources of water, and they became blood . . . Then the fourth angel poured out his vial on the sun, and power was given to him to scorch mankind with fire. Men were scorched with great heat, and they blasphemed the name of God, who has the power over these plagues, and they repented not to give him glory. Then the fifth angel poured out his vial on the government of the beast, and his kingdom was full of darkness, and they gnawed their

tongues for pain, and they blasphemed the God of heaven
because of their pains and their sores, and still would not
repent of their deeds. (Verses 4, 8-11)

God will send a scorching heat upon these same nations. Hundreds of thousands who have already been suffering will die now because they continue to defy God. They will not repent. Then, all light will be removed from these regions resulting in total blackness. This darkness will have the power to kill even more of these same hateful, rebellious people; yet they still will not repent. They will continue to curse God.

As with Pharaoh at the time of the Exodus in Egypt, man has a nature that seeks to do its own will, and this nature fights against yielding to God's perfect will. Mankind has always been this way. Mankind resists God, even to death, in order to hold onto his own self-rule, rather than yielding to God's rule in his life. Instead of repenting and seeking God, man tries to keep God out of his way.

John describes what he sees when the sixth plague is poured out, but it is the result of something that has already been underway for many months. The result of this vision, reveals the purpose accomplished by the sixth angel pouring out his vial. The purpose of this symbolism contained in John's vision was to bring these two superpowers together so that God could deal with them in one location. God has chosen to do this in order to bring about a final powerful blow to end all of man's self-rule. The result will serve as a future witness to the power and glory of God to end all wars—something that man could never do! Notice the description of the sixth angel pouring out his vial:

The sixth angel poured out his vial upon the great river
Euphrates, and the water was dried up so that the way
might be made ready for the kings to come from the east.

*And I saw three unclean spirits like frogs come out of the
mouth of the dragon* [symbolic of China and her allies],
and out of the mouth of the beast [symbolic of a United
States of Europe], *and out of the mouth of the false
prophet* [symbolic of the Pope of the Catholic Church].
*For these are the spirits of demons, working miracles,
who go forth to the kings of the earth and of the whole
world, to gather them to the battle of that great day of
God Almighty.* (Revelation 16:12-14)

Satan will actually exercise power and influence over all three
of these powers on earth, but there are demons who will do his
bidding, as this symbolism shows. Their influence will help bring
about the prophetic reality of this day when these two great
superpowers gather together for the *"battle of that great day of
God Almighty."* The result of the vial poured out by the sixth
angel will be that *"he gathered them together into a place called
in the Hebrew tongue Armageddon"* (Verse 16).

In the midst of all the confusion of this day, this war actually
will begin later in the day when the sixth vial is poured out.
Then, tens of thousands in these two armies will die in this all-
out confrontation.

The Seventh Plague

When the last vial is poured out, these two powers will stop
fighting each other. They will declare a quick truce because they
suddenly fear something much greater than each other:

*Then the seventh angel poured out his vial into the air,
and there came a great voice out of the temple of heaven,
from the throne, saying, "It is done!" There were noises,
and thunder, and lightning, and there was a great
earthquake such as there never has been since mankind*

was on the earth. The earthquake so mighty and so great that the great city [Rome—the seat of religious power over Europe] *was divided into three parts* [no longer a city of seven hills], *and the cities of the nations fell* [the great cities of both superpowers], *and great Babylon came in remembrance before God, to give unto her the cup of the wine of the fierceness of his wrath. And every island fled away* [prophetically symbolic of every smaller country seeking to escape, but could not], *and the mountains could not be found* [prophetic symbolism that all the great governments of these superpowers are destroyed—they no longer exist]. *And there fell on men a great hail out of heaven, and each weighted about a talent* [100 pounds / 45 kg], *and men blasphemed God because of the plague of the hail, for the plague thereof was so exceedingly great.* (Revelation 16:17-21)

This plague will be the final blow which will completely destroy all the remaining governing structure of both superpowers. The entire infrastructure of all these countries will collapse. This destruction will prove to be overwhelming; the death toll will mount into the tens of millions.

These two great armies will still be fighting each other as this last plague is being poured out. During this plague, they will stop fighting. Both will receive word of the scale of destruction in their home countries. They will no longer fear each other, but they will fear, what they now see, as the source of their demise. They will see the movement of that which will be glowing in the heavens. They will not understand what it is, but they will see it moving toward them. The next thing that will happen is unbelievable.

Uniting to Fight God

At the end of the Seventh Plague, Jesus Christ and the spiritual army of 144,000 new members of the God Family begin moving toward the location of these two great superpowers:

> *Then I saw heaven opened, and behold a white horse, and He who sat on him was called Faithful and True, and in righteousness He judges and makes war. His eyes were like a flame of fire, and on His head were many crowns. He had a name written, that no man knew, but He Himself. He was clothed with a robe dipped in blood, and His name is called The Word of God* [Jesus Christ]. *And the armies which were in heaven followed Him upon white horses, clothed in fine linen, white and clean* [the 144,000]. *And out of His mouth went a sharp sword, that with it He should strike the nations, and He shall rule them with a rod of iron. He treads the winepress of the fierceness and wrath of Almighty God. He has on His robe and on His thigh a name written, King of kings, and Lord of lords.* (Rev. 19:11-16)

Jesus Christ came the first time, as the Lamb of God to die as man's Passover, so that man could be saved through Him by the forgiveness of sins. The second time He will not come as a Lamb, but as a Lion; and He will not come in peace, but in war. The war He will bring will be swift and decisive, as He and the 144,000 will destroy the army of both superpowers. As it says, *"He treads the winepress of the fierceness and wrath of Almighty God,"* by destroying this final display of man's opposition to God. Now, all mankind will be fully humbled before God and God will usher in His Kingdom to reign on earth.

This final war will be swift and powerfully strong!

> *Then I saw an angel standing in the sun, and he cried with a loud voice saying to all the fowls that fly in the midst of*

heaven, "Come and gather yourselves together to the supper of the great God, that you may eat the flesh of kings, and the flesh of captains, and the flesh of mighty men, and the flesh of horses, and of them that sit on them, and the flesh of all men, both free and bond, both small and great." [he speaks of the destruction of this army and says that the birds eat their flesh once they are slain]. *And I saw the beast, and the kings of the earth, and their armies, gathered together to make war against Him that sat on the horse, and against His army* [these two opposing armies unite to fight against Jesus Christ and His army]. *The beast was taken* [leader of the United Europe], *and with him the false prophet that worked miracles before him* [the Pope], *by which he deceived them that had received the mark of the beast, and them that worshipped his image. These both were cast alive into a lake of fire burning with brimstone. And the rest were slain with the sword of Him that sat on the horse, whose sword proceeded out of His mouth, and all the fowls were filled with their flesh.* (Revelation 19:17-21)

In this final battle, over 200 million will die.

During this time period (three and one-half years) of this Seventh Seal, **over 6 billion** people will die.

Now, finally after 6,000 years of man's self-rule, God will rule the earth through His Son, Jesus Christ, and the 144,000 who then will be in the Kingdom of God—the Family of God:

And I saw thrones, and they sat upon them, and judgment was given to them [to the 144,000] *and I saw the souls of them who were cutoff for the witness of Jesus* [these had been cutoff from the world for holding onto God's way], *and for the word of God, who had not worshipped the beast, neither his image, neither had received his mark upon their foreheads, or in their hands. These lived and reigned with Christ for a thousand years. But the rest of the dead* [the rest of mankind who had lived and died throughout the first 6,000 years of man's time on earth] *lived not again until the thousand years were finished* [they will be resurrected to physical life once more, but they will then be living in God's world once the 1,000 year reign of Jesus Christ has ended]. *This is the first resurrection* [referring to the 144,000 who are in the first great resurrection of mankind]. *Blessed and holy is he who has part in the first resurrection, for on such the second death has no power* [the 144,000 have not been resurrected to physical life again in this first resurrection, but to spiritual life], *but they shall be priests of God and of Christ, and shall reign with Him a thousand years.* (Revelation 20:4-6)

This new millennial age for mankind will bring peace, equity, righteous judgment, prosperity, joy, and happiness on a level which will be so great that man cannot even imagine it.

Chapter 6

WHY SUCH MASSIVE DESTRUCTION?

The catastrophic events of the Seventh Seal will result in global destruction and the death of over 6 billion people. It will be the final three and one-half years of man's self-rule on earth, and it will end with the establishment of God's righteous rule for the next 1,000 years. This perfect world-ruling government of God will be led by Jesus Christ. The 144,000, who have been resurrected to serve as kings and priests in this government, will be ruling with Him in the Kingdom of God.

This great change in world government will not come easily. Naturally, the enormous death and destruction worldwide brings the following questions to mind. Why? Why does God allow this? Why does such a thing have to happen?

The answer cannot be given in a few simple sentences. The more you come to understand God's purpose and plan on earth, the more you can begin to understand "why."

Many will blame God for all that will happen. They will reason that if God is indeed all-powerful, why would He allow such a thing to happen to mankind? Couldn't He prevent all this? Some of this has already been covered in this book, but the greater answer needs to be examined more closely; then you can begin to more clearly understand God's infinite wisdom in the way He will save mankind.

God's Purpose for Man

If you truly want to understand why God will not prevent the horrifying destruction and death that will soon cover this earth, then you need to stop and ponder why we were placed on this earth in the first place. The specific answers of "why" this end-time destruction must come to pass will follow in the latter part of this chapter, once the plan of God is explained.

Do you know why you exist? Rather than seeking the answer from the One who placed us on this earth, much of mankind chooses to believe that he evolved from slime in the ocean, and that eventually, he began to crawl upon the earth. Then, over millions of years, he finally evolved into present-day man.

Mankind is so intent on keeping God out of the picture that he eagerly awaits greater evidence that he evolved. Man is determined to distance himself farther and farther from God.

Even for those who claim to be religious, the Biblical account of Adam and Eve seems too simplistic. Rather than God creating the first two human beings exactly as He said, some prefer to believe that He used some means of evolution to bring about the human race.

Even though many religious people find the story of Adam and Eve difficult to believe, they do like the idea that there is some kind of afterlife. Man doesn't like the idea of finality in death. He prefers to believe that there will be a continuation of life beyond death, but not the kind God has told man about.

Ideas of an afterlife among this world's religions are far too numerous to mention. Although mankind does not choose to believe God concerning such matters, he does like the idea of living beyond this temporary physical existence.

During the latter half of the past century, God worked through His Church to tell the world "why" man was placed on earth and the purpose of his existence. But the reality and the true witness is that **people did not choose to believe what they heard.** Instead, they choose to hold onto their own religious ideas and beliefs, which are false. Therein is much of the problem and much of the reason why man's self-rule must come to an end exactly as described in this book.

Rather than trying to prove to you in great detail how God's Church told the world about God's plan and how man rejected it, I will simply tell you the facts. However, more about how the Church did this is covered in *The Prophesied End-Time*.

God placed man on this earth as part of a very great plan He has for us. But because of his selfish nature, man has chosen not to believe God; and instead, he has chosen to hold onto fables and lies about his existence, as well as his future. Man has responded to God in this way because, as a result of his selfish nature, **he refuses to accept responsibility for his own actions.** The truth is: we are responsible for our individual actions. We will return to this later, since it is such an important part of the story.

God's purpose for man is awesome and exciting, but Satan and religious leaders, who have followed Satan's influence, have deceived mankind into believing foolish distortions of what is really true. When people come to truly understand the truth about God's plan and purpose for them (and come to see that it is truly "good news"), they will come to see that it is far better and greater than they could have ever imagined. As an aside, this "good news" is what God has been telling man for six millennia; but man has consistently rejected it—and God has allowed this!

In the Beginning

The next chapter of this book will be dedicated to the Almighty

God, whom mankind has **chosen** not to know. Although many religious people throughout the world believe they know the God of Abraham, they do not! Part of the reason why man must suffer to such an extent is because he has rejected the true knowledge of God in order to continue to hold onto his lies. Man must be humbled mightily before he will listen **to the truth!**

Here is the truth! . . . In the beginning was God. There was nothing else. Our inferior brains cannot conceive of such a thing. How can man, with such limited mental capacity, understand anything so vastly superior? He cannot! This is much of the problem. Man is so filled with vanity and pride that he actually believes he can understand such things. Therefore, he rejects what is true and develops his own ideas about God, which tend to pacify his inability to understand that which he cannot.

Man is limited in his mental capacity by the physical world around him. Tremendous technology has burst onto the world in the last century, yet in all this, man is still limited to the physical.

God is not physical. He is spirit. He is composed of spirit, and He dwells in a spirit world. His power and might is in His spirit—not in anything physical. God reveals that everything physical is actually sustained by that which is spiritual—by Him! The universe would not exist without God sustaining it! God created and sustains a physical universe by the power of His spirit that executes His will. How can a physical human being understand such things? On his own, he cannot!

God must reveal to man that which is spiritual. God uses things that are physical to teach about things that are spiritual, since man is limited to the physical universe around him.

Jesus Christ gave an example of this. Christ taught that spiritual life can grow and develop in human life (in the mind of mankind). Christ explained that He was the bread of life and that people would actually have to eat of His flesh and drink of His blood. For many of the Jewish students who had been following Him, this was too difficult for them to hear. They had always been taught that God forbids eating human flesh and drinking any kind of blood. Many stopped following Him from this moment because they could only think in literal, physical terms. Jesus was speaking of spiritual symbolism that the Church would later observe as part of the annual Passover service. In this service, God's people eat a piece of unleavened bread that represents the physical life (flesh) of Jesus Christ that He sacrificed for mankind, and the small amount of wine they drink represents His blood that He spilled (when He was killed) for the sins of all.

Many who consider themselves to be Christian do not understand this either, even though they think they do. Some take of the symbols of bread and wine and believe they are doing as Christ taught, but they are wrong; and they are actually disobeying what He explained. They do not understand what Christ was saying, so they soothe their minds with a counterfeit of Passover that they call "communion."

There is a way that the human mind can begin receiving true spiritual understanding, but the religions of the world (no, not even traditional Christianity) do not understand such things. Some of this knowledge will be given in the last chapter.

When man comes to the point that he will listen to God and begin to receive true knowledge of Him (which is explained in physical terms), then God will begin to share His spirit with mankind in order to give him the ability to begin "seeing" Him (in truth). Such "seeing" is spiritual in nature and requires that we be able to receive of God's spirit. When a human being "sees" something that is spiritual, it is not a matter of seeing something through the human eye; it is a matter of "seeing" in the mind (of the spirit).

So again, in the beginning was God. There was nothing else. Absolutely nothing! God has eternally existed in His eternal spirit. How can a temporarily-living, physically-existing, mentally-limited human being understand such things? Again, he cannot! God Himself must reveal that which is spiritual.

Without God, there is no life after death. A physical human being *can* understand this. After a person dies, we know what happens to the physical body. In time, it decomposes and fragments into the very elements from which it was composed. It returns to the elements (dust) of the earth just as God said. When a person dies, all life ceases, although some think a spiritual life continues.

Man doesn't like this finality, and he doesn't like what God tells him concerning life beyond physical death; so he has developed his own concepts of an afterlife. Over the centuries, these ideas have not given man much comfort; but they seem to help soothe the conscience.

The truth is: once man dies there is nothing else. He does not go to heaven and he does not go to hell. When man is dead, he is totally and completely dead. There is **no immortal soul** in man. This is a lie, and it is a false teaching of man. Rather than believe what God says, man has chosen to believe that he has a "soul," which is not physical, and can live on after death. That is a gargantuan lie that has been foisted upon man by false religious scholars and false teachers.

God told mankind that death is the penalty for sin, *"The wages of sin is death, but the gift of God is eternal life through Jesus Christ our Lord"* (Romans 6:23). And God adds that *"all have sinned"* (Romans 3:23).

If someone lives a wretched and wicked life, then dies, he does not have an immortal soul that is taken to some place of eternal torment or imprisonment. God says that the payment of sin is death, not being punished for eternity. Mankind, and especially traditional Christianity, has twisted the truth in this matter. God speaks of eternal punishment. Man has twisted that into eternal punishing. They are not the same! God speaks of a time of final judgment that will come on those who, in the final end, reject God. They will receive a judgment that will last for all eternity, and it is the punishment of death—never to receive any kind of life again. This is an eternal punishment, but not eternal punishing. More about this will be explained later.

God Began to Create

Again, in the beginning was God. God is an eternal being—the One and only Being of all eternity. You are limited in your understanding to the physical plane. You cannot begin to understand the great depth of such knowledge that is spiritual in nature. No one can. God reveals that all knowledge, all understanding, all wisdom, and all thought are from Him. In His Being, in His Wisdom, in His <u>Word</u> (Greek – "logos" – revelatory thought—which is the product of His Divine thinking), Almighty God determined to create that which did not exist. He set in motion a plan that would carry forward into eternity. He **predetermined** how His plan should be fulfilled.

Prophecy given to mankind is simply the revelation of God's plan and how it will unfold in actual events.

From the beginning, God was alone; but He was going to change this through a plan He would fulfill, in great patience, over millions of years. This plan began with the angelic creation.

God created angelic beings to share in this plan and to serve Him in carrying it out. These beings were created out of spirit, and they are spirit. God desired to share with the angelic realm His plan of much greater things to follow. God did not choose to make the angels like spiritual robots to function as programmed.

Instead, God created the angels with the capability of free, individual thought. They were created as individual, free moral agents who could make choices and express individual personality through those choices. This meant that they could choose not to follow God. They could choose their own way, living apart from what God told them was **the only true way** of life. This is a consequence of creating such beings. There is no other way to give life to beings who are capable of having "free choice" and complete individuality. Mankind also is created with the ability of free choice.

God knew that not all of the angelic creation would choose to live His way, which is the one and only true way capable of producing eternal peace—life that is happy, fulfilling, rewarding, and genuinely exciting. The knowledge of this phase of God's creation shows the great wisdom in why man was created physical and why man was created after the angelic realm.

The Angelic Realm

Multiple millions of angels were created. God does not give the exact number, but He does reveal that He created three angels who were superior to the rest in importance, might, beauty, authority, and power. These three are referred to by name: Michael, Gabriel, and Lucifer.

In time, after the angelic creation, God began to create the physical universe. Up to this point in time, only the spirit realm existed. The creation of the universe was exciting to the angelic family of God. God said that, upon seeing what He was creating, the sons of God (angelic realm) shouted for joy.

God said He created every thing in the universe in beauty and perfection. In time, God began to reveal more of His plan and purpose for the physical creation. God revealed to the angels that of all His physical creation (the universe), His plan would be focused upon the earth. God placed Lucifer on the earth, along with much of the angelic realm, to prepare for future events that He had predetermined long before.

Lucifer was placed in authority over the angels on earth, and they were to carry out preparations for even greater events in God's overall plan. God revealed to the angelic realm that He was going to create mankind and that the creation of mankind would lead to the ultimate purpose of all His creation. Mankind was going to be created with the potential of becoming far greater than the angels. God revealed to the angels that they would share in the joy of what He would create through mankind. The angelic realm was shown that they were created to share and help in this greater purpose of all creation.

Lucifer did not like what God revealed. He became lifted up in pride and his own reasoning. He chose to believe that God's way was not best, but that his own way was better. In his own perverted thinking, he rejected the knowledge of God and began to believe that his own way was so much better. He actually became deceived into believing that he could rise up against God and take over all rule of the physical and spiritual realm, making God subservient to him.

Over time, Lucifer planned and plotted. He began to spread his disdain for God's plan to other angels. As astounding as it is, a third of the angelic realm sided with him in a horrific rebellion against God. Lucifer would learn that he was puny before God, and indeed, God is Almighty!

The rebellion originated from earth. Lucifer planned to destroy the earth because he so hated God's plan, which was to be fulfilled here. Lucifer planned on ascending to God's throne and rule in God's stead. The solar system of our sun and the earth changed dramatically on the day of this rebellion. God tells us that, at this point, the earth became waste and uninhabitable, as all life on it was destroyed. The earth was toppled from its perfect orbit, and the atmosphere was filled with total blackness from the debris. A type of nuclear winter engulfed the entire earth in an immediate moment in time.

Even the moon and Mars were littered by the debris from this massive and explosive attack on God's physical creation. Although God limited Lucifer's attempt to destroy the earth and this solar system, He left the evidence of this attack for all to see—in time. The asteroid belt did not exist before this rebellion. God stopped the destruction of the solar system, and the debris was confined to this one region—not beyond.

From this time forward, Lucifer became known as Satan, the first great *adversary* of God. Satan chose to rebel against God and make himself an adversary of God and His plan and purpose. The angels, who rebelled with Satan, became known as demons.

God knew that some of the angels (having free moral agency) would, in time, rebel against Him and go their own way. Any way that opposes **God's perfect way** will lead to chaos, confusion, suffering, and every way that is evil. Turning from God's way of thinking results in pride, vanity and deep selfishness that is inward in nature and filled with the way of "get," while God's perfect way is the way of "give."

In all this, God knew the outcome! It was all part of His awesome and perfect plan that would continue forward, just as He had predetermined millions of years before. Holy righteous character cannot be created in any being who is given independent thought and personage. The way one lives life is always a matter of choice.

Although God knew there would be an angelic rebellion, the choice of **how** to live was, nevertheless, theirs to make. Those angels couldn't blame anyone else for their choices. God taught the angels that there was only **one true way** to live life. He also taught them that choosing any other way of life would produce automatic penalties. Those angels who chose to live God's way have shared in the joy of what God is working out in His plan for His creation. Those who have refused God's way and followed some other way have lived in futility—unfulfilled and never satisfied.

Lucifer and the demons who followed him are "set" in their ways. From the beginning of their disobedience, since they are spirit in composition and thought, they "set" themselves against God.

The Creation of Man

The next sequence in God's plan was the creation of mankind. Many who read the first chapter of Genesis believe they are reading about the initial creation of the universe. They are not! They are reading about the refashioning of the earth when life was placed upon it once more. The earth had existed for millions of years, yet without life, since the time of Satan's rebellion.

The first chapter of Genesis tells the story of God reshaping the earth to make it inhabitable, once again, so that He could put mankind on it:

> In *the* [a] *beginning God created the heaven and the earth. And the earth was* *without form* [Heb.—a place of chaos and waste], *and* *void* [Heb.—filled with emptiness], *and darkness was upon the face of the deep* [as a result of

Satan's rebellion, this was the condition of the earth at this moment in time, as God was preparing the earth for mankind]. *And the Spirit of God moved upon the face of the waters.* (Genesis 1:1-2)

The waters were already present, and God's spirit began to work upon the waters to make oceans, lakes, rivers, and the means for life on earth to once again be nourished by it. The story of the refashioning of the earth, and the creation of new life on it, continues in the verses that follow.

Then, God finally created the first man and woman. Why? What is God's purpose for creating physical human beings? It is an awesome thing to learn the purpose and plan God has for creating mankind. Yet, man has been ignorant of this great truth.

In the second chapter of the Book of Hebrews, the apostle Paul speaks on this same question, concerning the purpose of man. He refers to David (Psalms 8), who asked the question: "What is man that you [God] are mindful of him?" It is the kind of question that all should ask and want answered. Why are we here? Why did God create us?

The answer is given in these scriptures, and throughout the word of God, yet man has remained blind to the truth of it all. Paul repeats what David wrote and then explains that the angelic realm was created to help those who were to become heirs of salvation. But Paul goes on to explain that man was created to receive (inherit) something much greater than the angels.

Paul reveals here that God's purpose is to place mankind over all His creation. First, the description of man is that he is made (created) a little lower than the angels. Notice what is said about man:

> *You* [God] *have put **all things** under his feet. For in that He has put all things in subjection under him, **He left***

> *nothing that is not put under him. But we do not yet see*
> *all things put under him.* (Hebrews 2:8)

God reveals that His purpose for mankind is to become far greater than the angels. What is greater than the angelic realm? This is the amazing thing about God's plan for mankind that is so astonishing!

Paul explains that God's plan was to put "all things" under the feet (control) of man and that God "left nothing" that would not be put under his "subjection." God further reveals that this will not happen while man is in his present physical state.

Paul adds that *"we do not yet see all things put under him* [man]. *"* However, Paul does explain what we currently see concerning Jesus Christ, who was born a physical man. He states that Jesus Christ, as with all mankind, was made a little lower than the angels, and that His purpose was to suffer death for all mankind. Jesus Christ was the only human being that lived a perfect life in complete obedience to God. **All others** have sinned against God. Since Jesus Christ's Father was Almighty God, and since Jesus Christ lived a perfect life in obedience to God, He was able to be the perfect sacrifice for the sins of all people. Mankind could be saved through Jesus Christ—the Passover sacrifice.

Paul's account of how **all things** are "not yet" placed under man includes his explanation of what we can now see. We see Jesus Christ, who was made a little lower than the angels, by being made a physical human being, now crowned with glory and honor. Since this is God's ultimate purpose for all mankind, we see that Jesus Christ is the first one of all mankind to receive of this great purpose. It is revealed even further that God has put **all things** under Christ's feet. Indeed, God's purpose is to eventually bring all things under man's feet, but not in his current state.

Mankind, in his present physical form, is incapable of experiencing or exercising such power; and he could never be entrusted with such a thing (all of God's creation under him).

A Change in Man

Mankind does not know why God created him and placed him on this earth. However, we are now entering the time when God will begin revealing this great plan to everyone in the world. Man will begin to understand this great purpose. Some will begin to see this purpose as we approach the final three and one-half years of man's self-rule, and then, during that final period, multiple millions will begin to grasp the great plan of God. When this time is finished and Jesus Christ begins His rule on earth, everyone will be given this understanding.

The angels were created as spirit beings. They were given freedom of individuality. They had the power to think freely, learn and retain knowledge. They were free moral agents.

Man was created similarly, only physical. God gave man the same ability to think freely. Man was created a free moral agent—to think, learn, plan his own life, and make his own decisions.

Human life is a great marvel. We are unique in all the physical creation. In the animal realm, God made creatures to have instinct. They were not given freedom of thought with individual minds to think and reason. They were given limited mental capacity that functions primarily by instinct (preprogramming given by God).

Geese fly south for the winter; they do not have to think about it. Koalas are unique in that they sleep most of the time, and they are sustained by eating only Eucalyptus leaves. God simply made them this way. Great humpback whales migrate in the waters between Alaska and Hawaii, year by year; they do not think about their journey. God programmed them to do what they do. Nothing evolved in the animal realm. It is as God created it.

But mankind, like the angelic realm, is unique through the power of the mind (the power of free choice). In actuality, every human mind has a spirit essence. The mind is not like the other organs of the body, which function simply in a physical way. Many of the brain's functions are preprogrammed by God. For example, we do not control our heartbeats. However, the mind is unique. The power to think comes from a spirit essence that God gives to every human (for the purpose of free thought, expression and individuality). This is not to be confused with the holy spirit that proceeds from the mind of God, from His thoughts. Without this spirit essence God gives mankind, we would be like animals.

The spirit essence God gave us does not contain life in itself. So that we can understand, the closest thing we can liken it to is a computer hard drive or a memory chip. Without power, it does not have the ability to perform the functions it was made to perform. It simply remains a source of stored information. In humans, this spirit essence is where the intellect is stored. This spirit essence is where (how) we process everything we choose to do (individual thought that produces individuality).When we die, this essence ceases to function; but it contains (stores) every experience, memory and thought we ever had in our human experience. When a person dies, that spirit essence returns to God. It has no life of itself, but God can place it into a **new** body to live once again, with the exact mind that existed previously at death.

This is the exact process that will occur in the great resurrection which will take place at the return of Jesus Christ and the resurrection of the 144,000. Consider Abraham as an example.

Although he died many hundreds of years ago, God will give him a spirit body, at the time of this resurrection, and place in it the spirit essence that was in Abraham (which returned to God at Abraham's death). Abraham's mind and individuality will be exactly the same as when he lived long ago. Only this time, he will not have a weak, physical body, but a spiritual one.

God offers mankind something far greater than a temporary human existence. We were created as temporary physical human beings for a great and mighty purpose. It was a predetermined part of God's ultimate plan before anything was ever created.

So why are we here? Why did God create us as He did? What is His purpose for us? Let's return to the story Paul tells, describing God's purpose for the angelic realm (from Hebrews, chapter 2). He goes on to explain that man was made to become greater than the angels. Paul explains that Jesus Christ was the first of mankind to become greater than the angels, and that all things have been placed under His feet.

So what is greater than the angelic realm? What is God's purpose for man? Paul tells of this purpose when he shows how it has now been fulfilled in Jesus Christ, but not in the rest of mankind. All things have not **yet** been put under the feet of mankind. So far, all things have only been placed under the feet of Jesus Christ.

Man and God

The first chapter of Hebrews tells God's purpose for mankind. It is contained in what God reveals through Jesus Christ:

> *God, who at various times and in different ways, spoke in times past unto the fathers by the prophets, has in these*

last days spoken to us by His Son, whom [Jesus Christ]
He [God] *has appointed heir of all things, by* [through]
whom [Jesus Christ] *also He* [God] *made the <u>worlds</u>*
[ages]. (Hebrews 1:1- 2)

Paul is explaining how God has communicated with (worked
with) mankind through His prophets over the previous four
thousand years. Now, God is working through His Son, whom
God had predetermined (1 Peter 1:20) would be <u>the way</u>
(through Christ) that He would fulfill His plan and purpose for
all mankind in the ages to follow. God also predetermined that
Jesus Christ would be heir of **all things**—all things were to be
under His feet.

Who [Jesus Christ] *being the brightness of **His** [God's]*
***glory**, and the express image of His* [God's] *person, and*
upholding all things by the word of His [God's] *power,*
when He [Jesus Christ] *had by Himself purged our sins,*
sat down on the right hand of the Majesty on high.
(Hebrews 1:3)

God is showing He had predetermined that He would
accomplish His great plan for mankind through His own Son,
Jesus Christ. God predetermined that Jesus Christ would be in the
brightness of His own glory, would uphold all things by His
(God's) own power, and would be just like God.

In the following chapter, Paul expands this story to show
God's great plan for all mankind, which is centered in Jesus
Christ. Let's read it again.

*Y*o*u* [God] *made him* [mankind] *a little lower than the*
angels, and you crowned him [mankind] *with **glory and***
***honor**, and you did set him **over** the works of your hands.*
You [God] *have put **all things** under <u>his</u> [man's] feet. For*
*in that He has put all things **in subjection under him**, He*

> *left nothing that is not put under him* [man]. *But we do*
> *not yet see all things put under him.* (Hebrews 2:7-8)

Are you beginning to get the picture? God determined, before He began any creation in the spiritual realm or the physical universe, that in His time, He would create man, who would be made lower than the angels. Mankind would be made physical, but God also determined that, in time, He would work to bring about a change in man so that He could have all things in His (God's) creation placed under him (man), and that he (man) would also receive of the power and glory of God Himself. God determined that He would accomplish this great change in and through His own Son, Jesus Christ.

Let's return to the story in the first chapter of Hebrews. Paul has explained how Jesus Christ died for the sins of mankind and is now seated (a matter of power and authority) on the right hand of the Majesty on high (God Almighty):

> *And He* [Jesus Christ] *has been made so much better than*
> *the angels, as He has by inheritance obtained a more*
> *excellent name than they have. For unto which of the*
> *angels did He* [God] *say at any time, "You are my Son,*
> *this day have I begotten you?" And again, "I will be to*
> *Him a Father, and He shall be to me a Son?" And again,*
> *when He brought in the first begotten into the world, He*
> *said, "And let all the angels of God worship him."*
> (Hebrews 1:4-6)

What is greater than the angelic realm? It says that Jesus Christ was made better than the angels. It says that Jesus Christ was seated in power and glory right beside Almighty God. It says that the very angels of God were to worship Jesus Christ. Only God can be worshipped. Jesus Christ became part of the God Family—He became a God being.

Notice what God Almighty says of Jesus Christ:

But to the Son [Jesus Christ] *He* [God Almighty] *says, "Your throne, **O God**, is for ever and ever, and a scepter of righteousness is the scepter of your kingdom."* (Hebrews 1:8)

The Biblical accounts of the Kingdom of God are literally about the Family of God. When Jesus Christ returns to this earth in the Kingdom of God, He will return with 144,000 who will also be part of this Kingdom. The 144,000 are those whom God has molded and fashioned throughout the past six millennia, who have lived on earth as all other human beings. Now, however, they will be resurrected as spirit beings. They will no longer be physical, but they will be able to manifest themselves physically. They were made a little lower than the angels, but now they are greater—they too are members of the God Family—God beings, just as their elder brother Jesus Christ.

The truth about God's purpose for creating human life goes far beyond anything man has ever imagined, even in fiction; and so it is very difficult to believe this truth. God purposed that human life be only temporary. His design and purpose is that we be changed from mortal to immortal, from temporary life to eternal life. This transition (this phase of creation) is something that God will offer every human as a matter of choice. God's ultimate purpose for creating man is that he is to become a part of the very Family of God, in the Kingdom of God—a Kingdom of God beings. How will such a thing come to pass?

Why Man Was Made Physical

Now, one may ask, "Why didn't God simply create us as spiritual God beings and immediate members of His Divine Family?" The answer is: God cannot create righteous character in individual beings because living according to God's righteousness is a matter of choice.

Do you remember what happened to the angelic realm? If any being is given the power of independence with individual mental capacity, then that being also has the ability of free choice. Not everyone will choose God's perfect way of life, which is righteous behavior expressed in outgoing love and concern for others.

A third of the angelic realm rebelled against the perfect way of God. Those angels chose another way that was based on "get," not "give." God knew the outcome that would result from giving free choice to created beings, and it was for this very reason that God was not going to create members of a God Family as He did the angelic realm. If He had created God beings as He did angelic beings, then the eventual destruction and rebellion from those who would not choose His way would be catastrophic to His creation and Family.

To become a member of the God Family, God determined that everyone would be of the **same mind** as God Himself. They would need to be in full agreement with His one and only perfect way of life. For this to be possible, there would have to be perfect unity of spirit and purpose in life—all being of **one mind**, yet individual in personality and experiences. It would be similar to the differences we see in each other. How could such a thing be accomplished? This is the very essence of why man was created physical. Man would have to go through a process of change in order to ultimately become a God being.

God has revealed that the only way spirit beings can be entrusted as members in the God Family is by God reproducing Himself. Read the previous sentence again; this is what God is doing through mankind.

The angelic realm cannot reproduce. They are created beings. God created physical life that can reproduce after its kind. But in this process of each kind reproducing only after its own kind, each individual creature that is reproduced is different. Every one is unique. No two are exactly alike. No two human beings are exactly alike, yet all of us are human and can only reproduce that which is human. God has a plan to reproduce after His kind—the God kind—in the Kingdom of God, with each member being different (no two alike). All those of the God kind (in God's Family) will have unity of spirit, purpose and mind.

To become a part of the God kind, a complete transformation must take place in mankind. It must take place in the mind. It must be a complete transformation through a renewing of the mind (in the way man thinks). The mind must learn to be motivated by God's nature, not human nature. It is interesting to note that the Greek word for repentance means to "think differently." It is God's plan to help mankind to think differently than the way he does naturally. God plans for man to think as He (God) does, righteously. This is why mankind is told to *let this mind be in you which was also in Christ Jesus"* (Philippians 2:5).

It was necessary that man be made physical. Man was made subject to vanity, but what does this mean? God created man of physical matter. It can only produce temporary life. Man's life, without God, is futile and filled with vanity. God knew what physical human beings would do. God knew that humans would turn inwardly and become filled with vanity, filled with self—selfish. This is the base nature of man. Everything is inward, based on the way of "get." The apostle John summed it up perfectly by explaining that man's motivation is based on the lust of the eyes, the lust of the flesh and the pride of life (1 John 2:16).

An infant automatically learns these ways very early as it develops this selfish nature, a nature that pampers self. This is true when a baby is hungry and uncomfortable. This process simply continues to develop as we grow older. Everyone is inward and selfish by nature. Some may disagree, but that will not change the truth.

God gave us the capacity to do good and evil because He gave us free moral agency—free choice through independent thought. Our actions are choices we all make, and whether we choose to do good things or evil things, our nature is still selfish. This knowledge about ourselves can be an incredibly difficult thing to see and admit. **Every choice** produced from human nature is selfishly motivated.

There is a great difference in behavior between God and man. Man's behavior (motivation and actions) is always based on the way of "get," while God's way is always based on the way of "give." Man's nature is selfish, always toward self. God's nature is giving—always away from self. God's nature is one of "pure" love that is focused on the genuine benefit and welfare of others—always on the way of sharing.

God's end-time apostle and prophesied "Elijah to come" was Mr. Herbert W. Armstrong. He explained this basic nature of man in a way which can help a person begin to understand. He said that one of the best examples of human love that man can understand is that of a mother's love for her own child. It is a deeply-enduring kind of love that surpasses most examples of care and affection, which bind people together in a unique relationship of parent and child. But even in this example of a parent's love toward one's own child, there is still selfishness. Such love is limited. It is confined toward self—toward their "own" child. This love is not capable of being extended toward other children in the same way.

So, whether or not we like the truth that our nature is totally selfishly motivated, we must all face it. God will bring everyone to a time when they will have to deal with their own selfish nature. This is not an easy thing to go through, but it forces us to address the most basic foundational truths in life as to why we were made physical and why we are here.

The Choice of Life or Death

The purpose for human life is that God is reproducing Himself. The bottom line in all this is that, in time, all human beings will be given the opportunity to choose whether or not they want to be in God's Family. However, when the time comes, it will not be an easy transition.

We cannot become a part of God's Family with our current selfish nature because it is the opposite of God's nature. It is only through the experience of human life, of being made physical (as mortal human beings) with the selfish nature that such a life produces, that we can ever come to see (learn) what God is like when He begins to reveal Himself to us. It is only by this means that mankind can, eventually, be brought to a point where he can make such a momentous decision in life—whether he truly wants to become part of God's Family. Under man's current condition (state of life), he is incapable of making such an informed decision. God's plan involves bringing mankind to a time when each individual can make a more genuinely informed, objective decision concerning the most important choice in his or her life.

When this time comes, and for those individuals who make the initial decision to choose God's way of life, the transition from human nature to God's nature begins **a long struggle over time.**

This change does not come easily because the choice for God's way of life is not as simple as yes or no. It will include a mental battle against your human nature, but God will provide the means to fight this battle successfully. However, you cannot really understand this battle until you have entered into it.

Consider the time of life when entering puberty, the teen years, and finally, the transition into adulthood. These are not easy times. The struggle even continues throughout the various levels of maturity that can be attained throughout adult life. To receive what God wants for us, it will be far more difficult and far more complicated.

The decision to become a part of the God Family will not be forced upon anyone. It will be a choice. Please understand that life is not owed to anyone. If you only have life as a human being, then you have been given so very much. Human life is a **gift** from God. It should be recognized as such, but sadly it is not by most people.

Although, as I write this, I realize that there may be many on earth who possibly don't consider life to be such a good gift. Many are born into the wretched conditions of poverty, famine, disease, etc. However, these things are not God's fault. They are man's—the results of choices made by selfish mankind. God created the earth in beauty and abundance, and He gave mankind strong healthy bodies. Through his selfish nature, man has horribly polluted this world. Even the health of mankind has continually degenerated over the millennia because of disobedience to God. Every bad, oppressive thing in human life today is **the result of man's own actions**—the sins of mankind.

Again, human life is not owed to anyone. It is a gift from God, and without God, there is nothing beyond it. You live, and then, you die. It is the cycle of human life. If you live a full life, then you will have accumulated many experiences—some good and some bad. Your life is what you make it. You have only yourself to blame for the wrong (bad) choices made along the way. If God did not offer more, then this is all that there would be. You would live and then die.

Many people do not like the idea of such finality. They prefer to believe that there is life after death. And indeed there is, but not in the way man thinks or wants! Man has rejected what God has told him and most religions have adopted a concept of life that continues, whether you have been good or evil. These teachings include the idea that when people die they simply go through some kind of transition to another dimension as some sort of immortal being, never to die again.

Traditional Christianity teaches that everyone has an immortal soul that continues to live after death. This teaching is not true. It is an outright lie! Now, more than likely, this will make some people mad. But do you really think God cares if anyone gets mad over the truth? This is a great deal of the problem. People get mad at God because they do not like **His ways**. Something will have to change, and it will not be God.

Man has a temporary existence; he is strictly physical. He has no immortal soul. The word "soul" in scripture simply means life—existence. In Genesis, God says that he made animals living souls.

Many twist what God said about the kind of life He gave to mankind:

> And the LORD [Eternal] *God formed man of the dust of the ground, and breathed into his nostrils the breath of* life [Heb.–"life existing"]*, and man became a* living [Heb.–"life existing"] *soul* [Heb.–"creature, being"]. (Genesis 2:7)

Religious scholars have taken the term "soul" to mean an "immortal soul" that God placed in man, and man alone. Yet, here in Genesis, God shows that He made mankind a life-existing being.

It is clear that God did the same thing for other forms of life, as He created them:

> *And God created great whales, and every living* [Heb.–"life existing"] *creature* [Heb.–"creature, being"] *that moves, which the waters brought forth abundantly, after their kind, and every winged fowl after his kind, and God saw that it was good.* (Genesis 1:21)

The word "creature" in this verse is the same as "soul" in the previous example, where God was referring to mankind. Even translators of the Bible have tried to hide the truth in these matters in an attempt to keep the idea of a "soul" completely unique to man, saying that he has an immortal life dwelling within him. There are many other examples of animals that God gave a "living soul."

Therefore, being created a "living soul" has nothing to do with immortality. It only has to do with a living existence. There is a life that is a physical existence (temporary), and there is a life that is a spiritual existence (ever-living).

Man has only been given the gift of temporary, physical existence, but God's plan includes eventually offering him spiritual, ever-living existence. Once again, please understand that physical life is not owed to anyone and neither is eternal life, since it too is a gift from God. Obviously, eternal life is a far greater gift than physical life; but it also carries with it immensely greater responsibility.

In time, all mankind will be offered eternal life or eternal death. What does this mean? God gave to every human being who has ever lived the gift of physical existence. In His time, God will offer each person the knowledge of how they can receive the gift of eternal life in His Family, and then the choice to accept it. Those who do not choose God's way will not be given eternal life, but they will be given eternal death. It is a choice. Eternal life is not owed to anyone. The only way to receive eternal life is to come to the understanding that only God's way of life is true and right. Every other way brings sorrow, destruction, suffering, misery, and every evil that degrades life. There is only one way of life that produces genuine happiness, peace, prosperity, rich relationships, etc., and that is God's way of life—there is no other.

Lucifer did not choose this way and neither did a third of the angelic realm. Not all of mankind will choose God's way, and as a result of rejecting the true ways of God, these people will be choosing eternal death, since this is the penalty for rejecting God's way.

God's 7,000 Year Plan

This book has discussed the 7,000 year plan of God. It has focused on what is about to happen on earth as the result of mankind coming to the end of 6,000 years of self-rule, which God allotted him. Although the complete story is more involved, the remainder of this chapter will summarize (though condensed) God's purpose that is being worked out. Then, it will be explained "why" such horrifying events must unfold, as they will, at this very end-time.

God predetermined that He would reproduce Himself. He plans to have billions born into His God Family—the Kingdom of God. This plan includes creating mankind and, in time, offering mankind the awesome blessing of becoming part of His Family. The only way to become God is to be born human first.

It is a necessary stage of life that makes possible the impregnation of God's life, which, in turn, can lead to being born into spiritual (eternal) life as a God being. More of this process will be covered in the next chapter. It is a story that is thrilling beyond imagination. It is one that can only begin to be told in its greater fullness now.

From the beginning, God told man to populate the earth. Throughout the past six millennia, mankind has indeed populated the earth. Billions of people have lived and died. Those who have died **are still dead**. They have simply returned to the dust of the earth. However, there is the spiritual essence that God has retained (it contains no life in itself). God will give physical life once again, "in His time," in a great resurrection. That's right! God will resurrect all who have ever lived and died. They will be resurrected to physical life once again. God will do this at the end of the 7,000 years of man's allotted time to populate and live on the earth.

Mankind must learn that the way of selfish human nature is incapable of producing lasting peace, happiness, prosperity, and fullness of life. The way of "get" (selfish, pride-filled motivation) produces sorrow, pain, suffering, competition, envy, jealousy, greed, anger, resentment, bitterness, wars, oppression, disease, hunger, lust, opposition, sexual perversion, depression, crime, debate, etc. Only God's way produces all that is good and richly fulfilling, with everlasting happiness and peace in life.

Six millennia of man's self-rule is the proof and the true witness (testimony) of the ways of mankind. This is the reason why God gave mankind such a long time to experience his own way. This history will prove to mankind that all his ways have failed. Every government, religion, and civilization of man has failed. Those that exist now are failing, and all would end in self-annihilation if God did not stop it. With so much overwhelming proof, man will be better equipped and more easily able to acknowledge that all of man's ways lead to destruction (as Lucifer's did), and that only God knows the way to lasting peace and fullness of life.

Overwhelming proof (evidence) of man's dismal failure through six thousand years of self-rule, along with the following one thousand years of God's rule, which will serve as the ultimate contrast, will properly equip man to more easily acknowledge the perfect ways of God. As night is to day, so is man's selfish way to God's way.

The Great Resurrection
After the 1,000 year reign of Jesus Christ and the 144,000 God beings with Him, the seven-thousand year plan of God will come to a close. The allotted time for man to populate the earth will have come to a close. At this time a most awesome event will occur. Man has remained blind and ignorant of this great phase of God's plan.

All who have ever lived and died will be resurrected to physical life once more. There will no longer be reproduction of human life, but there will be a one hundred year period of time for man to live and be judged by God's way of life. Everyone will learn of God and be ruled by the same government which ruled during the previous one thousand years under Jesus Christ. There will be only one religion on earth; there will be only one government.

Every baby who died after birth and every child who ever died will be resurrected to live a full life. All who are resurrected will know the great Eternal God and His ruling Family. At this time, God will work to save mankind and offer him eternal life in His Family. Traditional Christianity teaches that God has been trying desperately to save the world. No, He has not! This is not the time for judgment and salvation to be offered to mankind. God intended to offer salvation only to the 144,000, so that they could reign in His new government at the end of man's self-rule.

In this great resurrection, everyone will be given life in a healthy, whole, physical body. Those who were young when they died will be given the same young body (but whole and healthy) as they had previously. All those who were old when they died will be given a whole and healthy body of middle age. People will be given the same features (but whole and healthy) as they had at death or middle age. They will recognize one another. Everyone's memories will be the same as if they had simply fallen asleep and were awakened.

This is an encapsulated version of the awesome plan which God has for all mankind. This plan is soon to be revealed far more fully to all mankind. An awesome world lies just ahead, but before that time comes, mankind will experience the worst time of tribulation the earth has ever witnessed. Thankfully, God will not allow this time to last for more than three and one-half years.

As we enter the next 1,100 years, salvation will begin to be offered to all of mankind. Everyone will have the opportunity to know God.

Over the past 6,000 years, only 144,000 people have been separated from the rest of mankind to be worked with personally by God; in order to be molded, fashioned and trained by Him, so that they could rule with Jesus Christ in His Kingdom. The 144,000, like Jesus Christ, will not live a second time in physical bodies. On the day that Jesus Christ returns to this earth, the 144,000 will be resurrected and given eternal life in spiritual bodies. This will be the first great resurrection. This is the subject near the end of the Book of Revelation which has puzzled those who have read it:

> *And I saw thrones, and they* [the 144,000] *sat upon them, and judgment was given unto them . . . and they lived and reigned with Christ **a thousand years**. But the rest of the dead* [all others who died over the previous 6,000 years] *lived not again until the thousand years were finished. This is the first resurrection* [speaking of the 144,000]. *Blessed and holy is he that has part in the **first resurrection** because **the second death** has no power over them, but they shall be priests of God and of Christ, and shall reign with him a thousand years.* (Revelation 20:4-6)

The 144,000 will be in the first resurrection. They will reign with Jesus Christ. Death will no longer have power over them because they have been resurrected to immortal life as spirit beings—God beings of the God Family.

A second death is possible only for those who will be resurrected to physical life a second time. They will be the only human beings who can die a second death. It will be during the last one hundred years that all who have ever died will be resurrected again to physical life. All will have the opportunity to choose and live God's way of life during this time. Those who choose this life, live it, and conquer carnal human nature (selfish nature) will have the same opportunity as the 144,000. They will be resurrected (changed) to immortal spirit life as members of the God Family in the Kingdom of God—as God beings. God's plan beyond this point, and on into eternity, is far beyond human comprehension. There is good news beyond the suffering of human self-rule. Thankfully we are almost there!

The Big Question

This brings us back to the beginning of the chapter. Knowing that this world is about to enter a time which will have enormous global destruction, in which billions will die, the big question is "Why?" Why will God allow this? Why will such a thing have to happen? Why won't God prevent it?

Simply put, mankind does not want God's way. People must learn what their selfish ways produce. Man has always rejected God, except for those few (the 144,000) through time whom God has specifically called, converted, and personally molded and fashioned to be among the first to enter His Kingdom. These are a unique group of men and women. They have fought far greater battles than those in the future will have to fight because their battles were fought during man's time of self-rule. The 144,000, who have conquered and overcome, have paved the way for all others who follow. The rest of mankind, over the next 1,100 years, will have things much easier. Over the past six millennia, the people of God have suffered great persecution from the rest of the world around them, even while fighting their own human nature, in order to develop Godly character.

The world will become thankful to Jesus Christ for all He has gone through to be their Passover sacrifice, High Priest, and King. People will also become thankful for the faithfulness of the 144,000 who have helped pave the way for them, so that they can more easily become a part of God's Family.

Yes, man has consistently refused God's way. People have rejected and refused His prophets and ministers because they have hated the message they were bringing. This behavior has been consistent for six millennia! Human beings want God to give them a different way, one that is more to their own liking and design. It just doesn't work that way! Only God's way works. All others fail.

It will be difficult for people to come to understand (believe) that their nature is adamantly rebellious against the truth of God—against the ways of God—against God! This will be especially true for those who consider themselves to be religious (who believe they already know God). Man is actually defiantly resistant to God. Our nature is so filled with pride and selfishness that it takes so very much to bring us to our knees—to humility—before our Creator.

I am God's end-time prophet, the one sent by the Almighty God to all mankind at this end-time. Even so, people will not listen and turn to God simply because I have written this book. People have not listened to God's prophets. They have not changed even though they were given the words of God. It is an age-old story!

God has given me the words in this book, but people will not readily receive them. They will resist God's truth because of their stubborn, haughty pride. As a result, they will have to endure great suffering until they are finally humbled (if they are humbled at all). This is the way it has been for 6,000 years. Because of such nature, people must suffer in order to learn the ultimate lesson for mankind—we are not capable of ruling ourselves. Given today's technology, if God did not step in now, it would only be a very short time before humanity would destroy God's creation, just as Lucifer did!

God is not responsible for the horrific evil we see in the world today. Had God not withheld technology from us, we would have already destroyed ourselves along with all other forms of life. Because we are so stubborn and filled with pride and will not accept this, God must allow us to prove this truth to ourselves.

Mankind is responsible for the destruction that will come upon the world, which will begin when the Seventh Seal is opened and the Seven Trumpets begin to sound. It will be at the end of this three and one-half year period, on the very last day, that God will intervene to stop the madness of humanity and bring an end to mankind's destructive self-rule. On this very last day, God will destroy the two great armies that will be destroying the earth.

A very merciful and loving God will bring an end to man's self-annihilation. Not only that, God also will move the spirit world to facilitate in limiting the great tribulation to exactly three and one-half years. God will speed along a natural course of events that would otherwise be spread over many more years of human suffering and torment, which mankind would bring upon himself.

Yes, God could prevent all of it, but mankind wouldn't learn anything! Actually, man would resist God's new government.

You may not believe any of this **now**, but you will come to believe all of it. You may believe at some point during the great tribulation, when you see the truth of this book come to life. However, most people will refuse to acknowledge the truth (giving in to strong, selfish pride) and die during this great tribulation. They will be resurrected in the last one hundred years when they will be given opportunity to once again embrace the truth. At that time, it will be difficult to refuse the truth, since people will be able to see a beautiful new world under God's rule. Sadly, human pride is much deeper than you can imagine.

It actually will take the horror of this coming end-time tribulation to bring people to the point where, finally, they will begin to acknowledge their own ways and become willing to honestly consider God's.

The process whereby mankind is offered eternal life in God's Family is not an easy one. A very merciful and loving God has exercised great patience with mankind to bring us to the time just ahead of us—the time for His righteous reign on earth.

Chapter 7

THE MYSTERY OF GOD REVEALED

In regard to the title of this chapter, many may ask the question, "What mystery?" Depending upon your religious background, you may not believe there is any mystery about God. You may believe that you know who God is.

The religions of the world have different ideas about God. Even the groups in traditional Christianity (denominational or nondenominational) have different ideas about God. This is obvious, since each believes that its God teaches mankind something different from all others. And, as we have already covered, each believes it is correct.

They are not! God is not divided. There is only **one** true God of all mankind, and He teaches mankind only **one** way, **one** truth and **one** faith.

In this chapter, I am going to tell you about the one true God—the God of Abraham. Many of you believe you already know Him. **You do not—not as you will be shown!** It is my hope that each person reading this has the courage to read the entire chapter before passing judgment. Whether you do or do not believe what you read here has much to do with whether you will have opportunity to live into the new millennial period that is about to be established on this earth.

Once again, it is my duty to tell you that what is written in this book is not my own opinions, ideas or prejudices, but that this is from Almighty God. Furthermore, I am to repeat that I am an end-time prophet of the God of Abraham and one of His prophesied end-time witnesses. You are not accustomed to hearing such things because God has not sent a prophet to mankind for nearly two thousand years, and God has **never** sent a prophet to speak to the whole world as He has given me to do now.

Every religion on earth has gone astray! Over the past several hundred years, mankind has continued to drift farther and farther away from truth about God.

All of Judaism is in error! They do not now know the God of Abraham.

All of Islam is in error! They do not now know the God of Abraham.

All of Christianity is in error! They do not now know the God of Abraham.

The only exception is God's true Church. As God foretold for the end-time, a great apostasy did occur in His true Church, and, as a result, God separated the Church from His presence because of their disobedience. However, God has awakened a remnant of all who were scattered, just as He said He would do, and He has brought them back into a true relationship with Him. All others who were scattered have now reorganized into over five hundred different groups. All have fallen asleep spiritually or have completely abandoned the truth (apostatized). They no longer have a genuine relationship with

God. They do not know most of what will be covered in this chapter concerning who God is because God reserved this knowledge to be revealed through His end-time prophet—me. God did this, in part, as a sign of who He is working through as one of the two end-time witnesses. This knowledge is for those who will yet be drawn by God, repent of their error and join the remnant to live on into the millennial period, either as one of the 144,000 or among those who will continue on in God's Church—in the Body of Christ.

The Great Deception

Over the past 6,000 years, it has not been God's purpose to reveal Himself to the world, however, throughout the next 1,000 years, God's purpose is to reveal Himself mightily to all mankind. This process is beginning, even now, through the pages of this book.

In the beginning, God revealed Himself to Adam and Eve. They rejected the knowledge of God, and thereby rejected God by deciding for themselves what was good and evil. They rejected the authority of God and established themselves as the authority to judge what was the best **way of life** to live. As we have already covered, everyone has chosen this same course by deciding for themselves what is best. This is the way of pride. Everyone is filled with the same spirit as Adam and Eve, judging for themselves what they will believe, yet always rejecting the truth from God.

God knew what Adam and Eve would do, just as He knew that all mankind would do the same. From the beginning until now, God began calling people **out of the world** (out from the ways of man) in order to reveal Himself and His only true way to them. God did this on an individual by individual basis. If you have not read the previous chapters, you will not be able to grasp all that is being revealed in this chapter.

Again, it must be understood as the most basic knowledge of God that God has a very specific plan for mankind, whereby He will offer eternal salvation to everyone—but in His own perfect time. Part of this basic knowledge is that God's plan includes letting man follow his own ways for the first 6,000 years on earth. Man was to rule himself by being allowed to choose his own ways, and because of man's selfish nature, he would always reject God's true ways. The only exception to this over the past six millennia is those whom God would call out of the world. God called these in order to train them to become part of His ruling government in the one thousand year reign of His Kingdom on earth.

This knowledge is basic and focal to God's overall plan and purpose for mankind's existence. This is why the seventh-day Sabbath of God is so very important to man. The seven-day week is a constant sign of God's complete plan for man. The first six days (first 6,000 years) were allotted to man to work and pursue his own ways, but the seventh day is God's. It is His time to teach man His ways and to reveal Himself to man. The seventh-day Sabbath pictures the next 1,000 years of God's reign that will come to this earth when Jesus Christ returns as King of kings. The loss of this basic knowledge and man's disobedience to observing the Sabbaths as God commands are the reasons man does not know the times in which we now live. This is the very reason why man is ignorant of the fact that God's Kingdom is about to be established on earth.

God knew that Adam and Eve, as well as all of mankind, would reject His true ways. During the first four thousand years, man continued to remain in ignorance of who God truly is.

God did reveal Himself to those whom He called out of the world, but even to those whom God called, He only revealed Himself in a progressive manner. Abel, Noah and other early prophets of God did not know God as well as Abraham knew God. God revealed Himself more fully to Abraham than he did to those righteous men who lived before him. Then, when God called Moses, He revealed Himself even more fully than He had to Abraham. As time passed, God continued to reveal more and more about Himself and His plan and purpose through the prophets. The farther into the 6,000 years allotted to man, the more God continued to reveal. However, the world did not understand or receive this truth. Only those whom God called could understand. The world has remained cut off from God since the time of Adam and Eve. The 144,000 have been called out of this world and have been able to come into a true relationship with God, as well as come to know Him and His ways.

Then, after four thousand years passed, Jesus Christ came to this earth to reveal His Father to all mankind. The world did not receive this revelation, just as God knew it would not. God did not send Jesus Christ into all the world, but only to those of the tribe of Judah—the Jewish people. There were ten other tribes of Israel that had been scattered into parts of Europe several hundred years earlier. They were not of Judah. This will be important to understand later in this story.

Judah rejected the words of Jesus Christ. They would not believe the truth about who God is. They believed they already knew God through their own interpretations of the Old Testament scriptures. Year by year, these Jewish people kept the Passover because they remembered how God led them out of Egypt and into a promised land of their own. They did not understand that the Passover pictured something far greater than deliverance out of a physical nation where they had been held captive. The Passover pictured the Lamb of God who would have to be sacrificed as man's Passover in order for man to be delivered out of a spiritual bondage—out of sin. Judah could only grasp the meaning of Passover on a physical plane as part of their history, but they could not see the Passover on a spiritual plane as part of God's greater plan for all mankind.

Judah rejected the true knowledge of God that they had lost long before Jesus Christ was born of the tribe of Judah. It is a most incredible paradox that the Jews rejected the very one God sent to them—His own Son, who was their Passover.

After the death of Jesus Christ, one of the greatest deceptions that Satan ever foisted upon mankind began to be revealed. Satan has always worked to fight against God. He has worked to keep mankind deceived. **One of his greatest deceptions** began to take shape in the middle of the first century, A.D.

Throughout Judea, the apostles began to teach people about God the Father and Jesus Christ. Everyone rejected this message except for a few that God began to call out of the world in order to train them for His future government. The apostle Paul was called by God to go to non-Jewish peoples. He traveled north and northwest into Europe, and these people also refused his message, except for those few whom God began to call out of the world.

It was at this same time that a man known as Simon Magus came into the picture:

> *There was a certain man named Simon who previously had been in the same city practicing magical crafts and astounding the people of Samaria, giving the impression that he was some great person.* (Acts 8:9)

Simon Magus was an intellectually-talented individual who

fancied himself as a kind of priest and prophet who practiced the arts of astrology and mysticism. He was received by many as a wise man, a prophet and a priest. Many people held Simon Magus in high regard and followed what he said because they believed he was from God.

In Samaria, some of these same people heard Phillip teaching about Jesus Christ and they believed what he preached concerning the Kingdom of God, so they were baptized. Simon believed much of what Phillip was preaching and he followed him, witnessing many of the signs and miracles that were done through him. All this fascinated Simon Magus. When Simon saw Peter and John laying hands upon those who had been baptized, he witnessed these people receiving the power of the Holy Spirit from God. Simon wanted this same power, and he offered the disciples money if they would lay hands upon him; but Peter chastised him, knowing that Simon Magus did not grasp what he had witnessed concerning what God was doing in His Church. Simon simply wanted the same power in order to be like Peter and John, but he did not want the truth the disciples were teaching.

After this, Simon Magus gave up his quest to become great among the disciples. Instead, he set out to reestablish his own influence over people by using mysticism and cunning deception, just as he had been doing before. He did this in order to be accepted as some great teacher who had received special powers from God, just like the disciples.

Two Branches of Christianity

Simon Magus became the father of one of the greatest deceptions ever foisted upon mankind. He set out to establish a counterfeit of what he saw the disciples doing. In order to accomplish his new pursuit of self-aggrandizement, he went so far as to take upon himself the name of the chief apostle to the Jewish people, Simon Peter. Since the disciples were establishing a church, he continued his great lie by establishing his own version of Christianity and a different church.

He began to mix his own ideas and past beliefs with what he had witnessed and learned from Peter, John and Phillip. It was from this very moment in time that a counterfeit of the true Church emerged on the scene. Two branches, both calling themselves Christian, began to grow. One would always be small, and it would always be rejected by the world. This small Church was the one, true branch because it was from God and it was sustained by His great power. It is the true Church of God.

The other branch was counterfeit and became filled with pagan rituals and teachings. It was established by Simon (Magus) Peter and it grew and flourished, becoming larger and more popular in the world. God's Church has never greatly flourished; it has not been popular in the world. Many are going to hate this knowledge about a counterfeit tree of Christianity because man resists the truth of God and seeks to hold onto his own ways which are false. It doesn't really matter who gets mad or who hates what is being said. Those with such attitudes are going to have a very difficult road to walk in the next few years before Jesus Christ returns. God is not concerned with the whimpering, irritated and puffed up egos of those who refuse Him and insist on following their own stubborn beliefs in counterfeit Christianity. All counterfeit Christianity is about to be destroyed!

This new church of Simon (Peter) Magus called itself Christian. The traditional Christianity of today has its roots in that great false church.

The true Church of God has continued from the day it began in 31 A.D. It had as its chief apostles, Peter and Paul. Peter was over the portion of the Church that was sent to the Jewish people and Paul was over the other portion that was sent to the gentiles. The Church of God has never been large. God never intended it to be large, since this was not the time for salvation to be given to the world. Only those called out of the world, who were to be trained to become part of God's future government (among the 144,000), were part of the Church of God.

However, the church that began to grow and become large was the one that Simon (Peter) Magus established. By mixing various beliefs of the truth he had heard from the disciples with the false teachings of other religions in the world around him, he made his counterfeit of Christianity attractive to many. Simon was quite clever, as were those who succeeded him, in devising a charismatic religion that would exercise great influence over the fears and superstitions of man.

Human nature does not want the authority of God to rule over it. Human nature does like to worship a god that appeals more to its own nature, one of its own devising, with its own structure of government and authority, along with the power to establish or reject doctrine, and the power to choose whom it wants to convey its ideas and represent its vision to others.

It is by this means that Simon Magus attracted people to his new-found religion. It would be beneficial at this point to consider some of the methods that Simon Magus and his successors used to counterfeit the true Church of God.

God commands man to worship Him on the seventh-day Sabbath. However, during Simon Magus' time, people had their false gods, and the most popular belief at this time concerned the various forms of worship that revolved around ideas of a sun god. The day for such worship was on the first day of the week—Sunday. This is the very means by which the first day of the week derived its name.

Several versions of sun god worship were being followed by different foreign people. In the early stages of this new religion, Simon and his successors adopted some concepts from several of these different nationalities, thus helping to merge them together into one that he called Christianity. Rather than observing the seventh-day command given by God, this new false church incorporated Sunday worship.

The priests of pagan religions loved to receive preeminence and adoration from others, and they loved to exercise religious and political control over the lives of the general population. Large numbers of people were attracted to such ceremony and pomp. People were drawn to the glitter of the wealth that was displayed in buildings, ceremonies and the attire of the priests. This new church followed these same practices, while the true Church of God did not!

God's prophets and ministers were to be shown respect for the position God had given them, but there was never the show of preeminence, grandiose, glittering ceremonies, or even the carrying of religious titles. The prophets and ministers of God's true Church were to serve in humility of spirit never accepting adoration of any form. However, this new false church disobeyed the word of Jesus Christ and took upon itself religious titles as it willingly received the adoration of the populace.

These are some of the very things that Jesus Christ condemned in the teachers of Judaism. God's representatives were not to be like them:

But all their works [Jewish religious teachers] *that they do is to be seen of men. They make their phylacteries broad* [this referenced apparel worn to signify their eagerness, above other people, to be reminded of the law of God, and their desire for people to see them as being more righteous than others], *and enlarge the borders of their garments* [an effort to make their garments appear different from others—to look religious]. *They love the uppermost rooms at feasts* [their motivation was to be seen by others as important], *and the chief seats in the synagogues* [they thirsted for power and authority over others]. *They seek special greetings in the markets, and to be called of men, Rabbi, Rabbi. But don't you be called Rabbi* [as a religious title] *for one is your Master* [religious title], *even Christ and all of you are brothers. Do not call any man your Father on the earth* [as a religious title], *for one is your Father who is in heaven. Neither are you to be called Masters, for one is your Master, even Christ. He that is greatest among you shall be your servant* [God's prophets and ministers are not to be served, but to serve others]. *Whoever shall exalt himself shall be abased, and he that shall humble himself shall be exalted.* (Matthew 23:5-12)

The counterfeit Christianity adopted the practice of the false priests of the pagan religions and that of the teachers of Judaism. They did not adopt the religious title of Rabbi since that was fully Jewish in origin. Instead, they eventually incorporated titles of Father, Reverend and Pastor. The chief title of this new religion belonged to the one who was considered to have preeminence over all others, and that title was Pope [the Father of all Fathers].

God's servants do not use religious titles that belong to God. They do, however, have job descriptions that identify their specific service to God. Some are apostles, prophets, evangelists, pastors, elders, etc., but these descriptions are never to be used as a religious title or personal greeting (address or acknowledgment to be received from others).

Other Deceptions
There are only two branches, known as Christianity, that have their roots in the first century A.D. One is the true Church of God that has always existed since it began in 31 A.D. This Church has always carried the identity to whom it belongs—God. The other church is the Catholic Church. No other churches can be traced back to this beginning in the first century. All other churches have either split off from the true Church of God after abandoning the truth, or they have splintered off from the Catholic Church to form their own organization (or from some other such splinter). Some of these churches that exist to this day include: the Lutheran Church, Church of England, Baptist Church, Methodists, etc. Furthermore, the earliest of these didn't form until the sixteenth century, A.D. Therefore, it took nearly 1,500 years before any other group emerged that called itself Christian.

The list of counterfeit teachings is far too long to address here. Another book would need to be written. There are numerous pagan teachings that have merged into a framework, mimicking parts of Christianity. Some of the teachings of paganism that involved sun god worship included the birth of a son to a virgin mother. Satan knew God's plan of a future Son and counterfeited it long before the time of Jesus Christ. Statues of a mother and child being worshiped by followers of paganism existed for centuries before Jesus was born. Indeed, statues and other religious relics have always been a part of pagan worship.

In pagan worship, as part of a great religious observance that celebrated the birth of a son to the sun god, was the celebration of the winter solstice somewhere in the time period of late December to early January. Hence, it was not a difficult thing to counterfeit this pagan teaching by saying that this was the time of Jesus' birth, and thereby merge a semblance of the two religions. However, nearly all "religious scholars" will acknowledge that Jesus Christ was not born in this season of the year, but at a time nearer September. Some people get upset and ask, "What does it matter as long as Christmas is about honoring and worshipping Jesus Christ?" It is wrong because it is not from God. **All religious worship and observance is to be done exactly the way God commands.** God further commands that we are not to add to, or take away from, what He commands us. Doing things **our way** instead of **God's way** is the very problem that has existed since Adam and Eve, and this is the very thing which God is about to correct on this earth.

Another great deception concerns the teaching of a doctrine that has its origin in the false teaching of Easter. This topic will serve as part of an introduction into the content for the remainder of this chapter, regarding the mystery of God that is being revealed. It is helpful to understand the great deception that surrounds this false doctrine so that you might be able to begin to see what is actually true and what has held traditional Christianity captive for centuries.

By 325 A.D. the Catholic Church had become very strong, and it had great religious appeal among the populace as well as leaders in government. The Council of Nicea was called by the Catholic Church to address some foundational doctrines of their church that would carry powerful influence over all who would follow this same false course, even among the later splinter organizations.

The true Church of God, at this time, had remained small and was hated by others in the Catholic Church. Up to this time, and ever since, this great false church has been the primary persecutor of God's Church and has been responsible for the slaughter of many of God's people.

This information may be hard for you to hear, but you must come to grips with this knowledge now or you will have to do so in your resurrection after the thousand-year reign of Jesus Christ. God is not playing games with the world. Mankind will no longer be able to simply ignore God and continue on his merry way. God is bringing this great false system to a close! It will be destroyed, and all organizations that have copied it will be destroyed as well.

Notice what God actually has to say about this great false church and all who have been born of her teachings:

> *Then one of the seven angels which had the seven vials* [this is one of the angels that had one of the vials of the seven last plagues, which will be poured out on the very day of Christ's return] *came to me and talked to me, and said to me, "Come here and I will show you the judgment of the great whore* [God uses this term to describe her great spiritual whoredom used to deceive and attract people to a false religious system that calls itself of God] *who sits upon many waters* [a description of power, political influence and control], *with whom the kings of the earth have committed fornication* [spiritually], *and the inhabitants of the earth have been made drunk with the wine of her fornication* [people have been seduced and

made spiritually drunk on her false whorish ways]. *" So he carried me away in the spirit into the wilderness, and I saw a woman* [Catholic Church] *sit upon a scarlet colored beast that was full of names of blasphemy, and having seven heads and ten horns. The woman was arrayed in purple and scarlet color, and decked with gold and precious stones and pearls* [this church has always had great wealth], *having a golden cup in her hand full of abominations and filthiness of her fornication. On her forehead was a name written, MYSTERY, BABYLON THE GREAT, THE MOTHER OF HARLOTS AND ABOMINATIONS OF THE EARTH* [the harlots are all other churches that have their roots in the Catholic Church] *And I saw the woman drunk with the blood of the saints, and with the blood of the martyrs of Jesus* [responsible for the death of many of God's people], *and when I saw her, I was amazed with great astonishment.* (Revelation 17:1-6)

If you are beginning to see a bit of the picture, you will see that God is getting ready to finally bring an end to this great whore and all her harlot daughters. Does anything calling itself of God or Christian carry any weight with God if it is formed in disobedience? No!

Many of the harlot daughters of the Catholic Church think they are fully separate from her, but they are not. They do not grasp that their roots are deeply embedded in her. Before we continue with the importance of the Council of Nicea, it is first needful to describe a few of the false beliefs originating from the Catholic Church.

Some of the most hideous teachings of the Catholic Church, which hold traditional Christianity in captivity to deception, are focal to most of these religious organizations. I will mention a few of these false teachings and explain what is actually true.

The seventh-day Sabbath has been perverted into a doctrine of Sunday worship. Easter is observed instead of the Passover, which was replaced by the Council of Nicea. Christmas, Halloween, Lent, and Communion all have their roots in paganism and have been instituted to replace God's annual Holy Days. The truth about a future resurrection to physical life once again in God's world has been replaced by ideas of an immortal soul that goes to either heaven or hell at death (or some place between).

Jesus Christ said that the only sign He would leave that would prove He was who He said (the Messiah and man's Passover) is that He would be dead and in the heart of the earth for three days and three nights. He died late Wednesday afternoon and was placed in the heart of the earth just before sundown on that day. He was resurrected exactly three days later on late Saturday afternoon, just before sunset. So when the two Marys came to His burial site before sunrise the following morning, the angels told them He had already risen. But the Catholic Church has taught the world that Jesus died on "Good Friday" and was resurrected on early Sunday morning. Both are a lie! This would mean Jesus Christ was not our Passover sacrifice and that He is not the Christ, since they teach He was only in the heart of the earth for a maximum of two nights and one day.

Another great false teaching, which will be covered more in the subject of the Council of Nicea, is that God is a Trinity. It is taught that the holy spirit is a separate spirit being. This too is a lie! The holy spirit is the power of God. The Trinity is a kind of spiritual Three Musketeers stating that the Father, the holy spirit, and Jesus Christ are eternal beings who each are separate and yet are one. It is a great mystery because there is no truth in it. The awesome truth about God, which has been a mystery to mankind, will be fully revealed in this chapter.

Any religious groups holding to any of these false doctrines are themselves false! They received these false doctrines from the Catholic Church. Easter is nowhere mentioned in the Bible. The Mass of Christ (Christmas) is nowhere mentioned in scripture. The Trinity is not mentioned in the Bible anywhere, and neither are any of these other false doctrines I have mentioned. They are fables of the Catholic Church and God condemns them all. God is getting ready to destroy every false religion and everyone who insists on holding onto them. If you have any desire to live into the new world that is coming, then you must repent of these false doctrines you have been embracing.

The Council of Nicea
In 325 A.D., the Catholic Church convened the Council of Nicea. I will simply cover the highlights of this momentous event.

The Passover was in controversy and the Catholic Church wanted to be rid of it, since it wanted to be fully separate from all ties that associated it with the true Church of God, which faithfully observed the yearly Passover. It also wanted to distance itself from Judaism. The annual observance of Passover was replaced with the observance of Easter, which itself was rife with pagan practices (eggs, rabbits, fertility, hot cross buns, sunrise worship of the sun god, the resurrection of Tammuz, and the queen of heaven—Ishtar and Ashtoreth).

God did not establish a holy observance for the resurrection of Jesus Christ, but only for His death in the observance of the yearly Passover. The Catholic Church even perverted the

Passover observance by instituting weekly Communion. The taking of a piece of unleavened bread and the drinking of a small amount of wine is a yearly observance God commanded His Church, called Passover, which represents the religious significance of Christ's broken body and the blood that He poured out for our sins.

By substituting Easter for Passover, the Catholic Church was also attempting to give credibility to Sunday worship rather than the seventh-day Sabbath. By observing Easter and saying that Jesus Christ was resurrected at sunrise on a Sunday morning, it could then say Christ should be worshiped on Sundays. But as it has been stated, Jesus Christ had already risen before Sunday even began. He was resurrected just prior to sundown on the seventh day, before the first day of the week began. God gave man the method of how to count a day, counting from the moment of sundown of one day to the moment of sundown of the next. As an example, throughout the Bible the weekly seventh-day Sabbath was always observed from sundown on the sixth day (Friday) to sundown on the seventh day (Saturday). The early Greeks and Romans used the method of counting a day from midnight to midnight.

Not only did the Council of Nicea seek to destroy the true identity of Jesus Christ by instituting Easter, it also sought to destroy knowledge of the true identity of the Eternal God by instituting the perverted, sick and damnable doctrine of the Trinity. These two doctrines have been Satan's greatest and most fruitful attempts to deceive mankind into greater ignorance of who Jesus Christ and God the Father are. The identity and revelation of who the true Jesus Christ is was covered in *The Prophesied End-Time*.

The true Jesus Christ is not the one pictured with long hair, hanging lifelessly on a cross that the Catholic Church has deceived people into worshipping. Jesus Christ is God and He did die for our sins as our Passover, but He is very much alive and He exercises great power within the Church. He is about to return as His name Messiah (Christ) means, as the King of all kings who will reign for 1,000 years on earth over all mankind.

The God of Abraham

The books of the Bible were written over a long span of time. Through Moses, God recorded the events of the creation of Adam and Eve, on through the time of Noah and the flood, and on into the events that led up to the calling of Sarah and Abraham. The life of Abraham was covered earlier in this book as the story of two of Abraham's sons unfolded—the story of Ishmael and Isaac.

Then the story of Moses' calling was recorded, which surrounded the events of the Exodus out of Egypt. The first five books of the Bible cover this full span of time from Adam to the death of Moses. As time progressed and God continued to inspire more books of the Bible to be written, God gave increasing knowledge about Himself and His plan for mankind. After hundreds of years of written record given through the prophets, God sent His Son into the world. The events of the life of Jesus Christ, and those things He taught, are recorded primarily in the books of Matthew, Mark, Luke, and John. Then, less than seventy years passed when the final book was written by John—the Book of Revelation. It was written a little over 1900 years ago.

As the books of the Bible grew in number, so did the revelation of the knowledge of God increase. Yet most of that knowledge remained a mystery to man, except for those whom God called. From the very beginning, God increasingly revealed more about Himself to His people (those whom He called).

Through time, very few (only those who were called) were able to come to know God. To all others, God remained a mystery, even to the nation of Israel. Although God had called Israel out of Egypt, as a physical nation through whom He would work out much of His plan, Israel was not given the spirit of God, whereby it might truly know Him.

Since man, by nature, rejects the true knowledge of God, only those whom God called out of the world could accept Him and come to know Him. The words of God that are recorded in scripture are not able to be understood by simply reading or by one's own intellectual interpretations. Therefore, man has been unable to know who God truly is.

God reveals His words, and therefore Himself, through the power of His spirit to those whom He calls. God communicates directly with them, to their mind, through the spirit essence He has given to mankind. God is not limited to communication by means of the written word or vocal language. When people hear God's words spoken to them, or when they read them, the only way to understand (in spirit and truth) is if God grants the *hearer* the power of revelation from His spirit, which is communicated to the spirit essence in their mind.

So only those whom God has called have been able to truly understand what God has recorded and who God is. As time has progressed, God has continued to reveal more to His people, but not to the world. However, we are now entering the time when God is going to begin doing just that—reveal His will and purpose to all mankind.

So who is the God of Abraham?
After the flood, mankind began to repopulate the earth. Over three hundred and fifty years after the flood, God decided to call

Abram (Abraham), who was of the lineage of Shem (one of Noah's sons). Noah taught Abram about the ways of God, and as God worked with Abram he learned to obey God. God chose this one man (Abraham) through whom He would raise up a nation of people to help fulfill His purpose for mankind. The most important part of this purpose would be the birth of Jesus Christ who descended from Abraham:

> *Now the ETERNAL ONE* [translated often as LORD or JEHOVAH] *said unto Abram, "Get you out of your country, and away from your relatives, and away from your father's house, into a land that I will show you. And I will make of you a great nation, and I will bless you, and make your name great."* (Genesis 12:1-2)

God worked through the lineage of Abraham, Isaac and Jacob. It was Jacob's family who moved into Egypt during a time of great drought, and there they remained for four hundred and thirty years before God finally delivered them through the great Exodus. By this time, the people of Abraham, Isaac and Jacob had grown to a size of approximately six million people. They had become enslaved by the Egyptians. They had grown into a nation of people and now God was going to work with them in this very way—as a nation. God had changed Jacob's name to Israel, and this nation would carry his new name.

God told Abraham He was going to make of him (Abraham) a nation of people through whom He would work. The time had come for God to separate this nation as one people, and He groomed Moses for this task.

It is at this point that God chose to begin to reveal more about Himself as the God of Abraham. God began to reveal, from this period of time, His purpose for working through a nation of people that He had determined would come through Abraham.

The very knowledge God revealed about Himself, during this time, is the very knowledge that is rejected by others. The three religions of the world—Christianity, Islam and Judaism—which have their roots in Abraham, all reject this knowledge.

Even God's own Church, during the time of the Philadelphia era (1936 to 1986), did not fully understand all that God has revealed at this time.

There is no need at this time to go into further explanation of what I am about to say, although more will be given. But to put everything in the most basic terms, you need to be bluntly shown why man is ignorant of the true God of Abraham.

Simply stated, Judaism rejects the **Passover** that was revealed during this time, and therefore, does not know God. Islam rejects **Israel** (which is not only about modern-day Israel) and God's purpose for working through this nation, so it does not know God. Traditional Christianity rejects the Eternal One as the **one** true God, and therefore, it does not know God or His purpose for mankind.

Having read this, you may **believe** it isn't true due to your faith (beliefs), and if this is the case, then this is your problem! If you will exercise a little patience and continue reading, you may begin to understand and come to see the true God of Abraham.

There is so much confusion today about the true identity of God. Regarding the example just mentioned, the whole world has rejected the true knowledge of Israel, even those who identify themselves today as the nation of Israel. They are not the Israel of the Bible. The modern-day nation of Israel is primarily made up of the ancient nation of Judah—the Jewish people. Actually, the first time where Jew is mentioned in the Bible, it says they were at war with Israel. How is this possible in light of the present-day belief of all three major religions (Christianity, Islam and Judaism) that the Jews are Israel? Notice the evidence:

> *Ahaz was twenty years old when he began to reign, and he reigned in Jerusalem* [over Judah] *for sixteen years, but he did not do that which was right in the sight of the ETERNAL his God like his father David had done.* [Jerusalem was the capital city for the nation of Judah] . . . *Then Rezin, the king of Syria, and Pekah, the son of Remaliah,* **king of Israel**, *came up to Jerusalem to war* [**against Judah**] *and they besieged Ahaz, but they could not conquer him. At that time, Rezin, king of Syria, recovered Elath for Syria, and drove the **Jews** from Elath. Then the Syrians came to Elath and they have dwelt there unto this day.* (2 Kings 16:2, 5-6)

After the reign of King Solomon (David's son), the nation of Israel separated from the nation of Judah. From this time forward, each nation had its own kings who reigned over them. The nation of Israel was conquered by the Assyrians (Germanic people) in 722 B.C., and Judah was later conquered by Babylon around 586 B.C.

The nation of Judah remained captive for seventy years in Babylon, at which time they began to move back to Jerusalem and the land they had previously occupied as Judah. The nation of Israel was moved into regions of western Europe after their captivity by Assyria, and Assyria repopulated their land with the people of Samaria.

The nation of Israel would no longer be known by this name. They became known as the lost ten tribes of Israel. The nation of Judah was primarily composed of two tribes, Levi and Judah, and today these people are known as the Jews, regardless of where they live in the world.

But the ten tribes that make up the single nation of Israel are unknown by the world today because the world is ignorant of the God of Abraham and all that He has shown concerning His plan which is still being worked out in this world—much of which is through those lost ten tribes. The reason this book and *The Prophesied End-Time* have so much to say about specific events that will take place in the United States, Canada, New Zealand, Australia, the United Kingdom, and much of western Europe is that these nations are very specifically identified as the descendents of those lost ten tribes of Israel! End-time events focus first on the demise of these nations over the next couple of years. These events have everything to do with knowing the true God of Abraham.

How can people know God if they reject what He tells them? It is like listening to someone explain who they are, but insisting that everything they say about themselves is not true.

When anyone comes to **know** someone else, they do so as the thoughts (the thinking) of the other person begin to be shared through their speech and actions. The sharing of the contents of our minds reveals **the way** we are, and this sharing identifies each one of us as unique and individual. But if we reject what we see in another's actions and we do not accept what is true concerning the thoughts they share with us, then we can never really come to know them. Certainly, we would not be able to have any meaningful relationship with them. And so it is with man toward the Eternal God—the God of Abraham.

The God of Abraham Revealed

As God was giving Moses charge to lead Israel out of Egypt, He began to reveal more about Himself and His purpose for mankind. Before God began to reveal His purpose, He first began to reveal who He was:

God [Hebrew –"Elohim"–uniplural word for God] *spoke to Moses, and said to him, "I am the ETERNAL ONE* [Hebrew –"Yahweh" means the self-existing one and is often translated as LORD or JEHOVAH]. *I appeared to Abraham, to Isaac, and to Jacob, by the name of God Almighty* [**Hebrew –"El Shaddai"**], *but by my name the ETERNAL ONE* [Yahweh – the self-existing one] *was I not known to them."* (Exodus 6:2-3)

All the names for God are important; they reveal much about God and His purpose for mankind. All of these will be explained, but it is important to note here that God progressively reveals Himself as He progressively reveals His will to mankind. Abraham knew God as "El Shaddai," which means God Almighty, because this is how God revealed Himself. To Moses and all the children of Israel, God added that He was "Yahweh"—the ETERNAL ONE. Abraham, Isaac and Jacob did not know God as "Yahweh." God explained more to Moses:

I will take you to myself for a people, and I will be God [Elohim] *to you, and you shall know that I am the ETERNAL ONE* [Yahweh] *your God* [Elohim], *who brings you out from under the burdens of the Egyptians. I will bring you into the land concerning which I did swear to give it to Abraham, to Isaac, and to Jacob, and I will give it to you for an inheritance* [possession]. *I am the ETERNAL ONE* [Yahweh]. (Exodus 6:7-8)

The Eternal God was making it clear to Moses that He was going to take the people of Israel to Himself and be God to them. He was not going to be God to the rest of mankind, in the sense that He would work with them in a special way to accomplish His future plans. Certainly He was God of all mankind, but God was not working out His plan (at that time) in the rest of mankind. Instead, all the rest of the world would be allowed to continue on their own path, choosing their own governments and religions—choosing their own ways.

Although God chose to work with Israel as a nation, in order to fulfill His plan for mankind, Israel did not accept the rule of God and His ways of life. Some have been jealous of what God says about Israel because they have not understood why God worked with them as He did. Other peoples of the world have misunderstood much of what was being worked out through Israel, in order for the rest of mankind to learn from it. Much of the lesson of Israel is not a good one. God gave them His laws, but they rejected those laws and rejected God by doing so. Israel proved that even when given every advantage, intervention and favor in life from Almighty God, man still rejects God.

God Almighty (El Shaddai) was now beginning to fulfill some of those things He had promised to Abraham hundreds of years earlier concerning his descendents through Isaac and Jacob. Earlier, God had revealed other information concerning Himself:

Moses said to God [Elohim], *"Behold, when I go to the children of Israel and say to them, 'The God* [Elohim] *of your fathers has sent me to you,' and they shall say to me, 'What is his name?' What shall I say to them?" God* [Elohim] *said to Moses, "I AM THAT I AM." Then He said, "This is what you shall say to the children of Israel, 'I AM has sent me to you.'" Moreover God* [Elohim] *said to Moses, "This is what you shall say to the children of Israel, 'The ETERNAL ONE* [Yahweh], *the God* [Elohim] *of your fathers, the God* [Elohim] *of Abraham, the God* [Elohim] *of Isaac, and the God* [Elohim] *of Jacob, has sent me to you.' This is My name for ever, and this is My remembrance to all generations."* (Exodus 3:13-15)

The translation into English of the first thing that God told Moses to tell the Israelites is rather awkward. The translation of "I AM THAT I AM" does not really capture the greater intent of what God said. In English, it is better understood as, "HE EXISTS WHO EXISTS" or "HE IS WHO IS" has sent me to you.

Then God instructs Moses to say to the Israelites that the ETERNAL ONE (Yahweh), who is the God of their forefathers (Abraham, Isaac and Jacob), has sent him to them. Furthermore, God made it clear that His name, ETERNAL ONE (Yahweh), was to be remembered for all generations. Another way of saying it is that God is to be known to (remembered by) all generations as the ETERNAL ONE (Yahweh).

God, the ETERNAL ONE

As previously stated, the Hebrew word "Yahweh" means the Eternal One or the Self-Existing One. The key word in all this is "One."

As the most basic core of their belief about God, Judaism and Islam believe that there is one God! They both believe that there is only one God who is eternal, who has eternally existed. However, traditional Christianity has never believed this about God.

The basic faith (belief) of traditional Christianity is the Trinity. The Catholic Church established this doctrine during the Nicene Council in 325 AD. This is the same Nicene Council that changed Passover to Easter.

The Nicene Creed states the belief that the Father, Son and Holy Ghost are one God; yet it also states that each one is separate and eternal. This Nicene Creed, which establishes the doctrine of the Trinity, teaches that the Holy Ghost (spirit) is a separate eternal being of a single triune God. These people do not understand that the holy spirit is simply the power of God. God is spirit, and He uses His spirit to do His will. It is His power, and it is subject to Him. It is holy because the source is God Almighty. The holy spirit is not a living being.

Notice how the Trinity doctrine begins:

> We worship one God in Trinity, and Trinity in Unity; neither confounding the persons; nor dividing the substance.

The Trinity does, however, confound the truth about God. It continues:

> But the Godhead of the Father, of the Son, and of the Holy Ghost, is all one: the Glory equal, the Majesty co-eternal.

The Trinity teaches that all three beings share glory equally and all three are eternal. But to keep with the theme of a trinity, the doctrine also states:

> And yet there are not three eternals, but one eternal.

The Trinity teaches that the Father is a separate being of this single triune God and that He has eternally existed. This teaching is also saying that the Son (Jesus Christ) is another of these three beings of this single triune God and that He too has eternally existed.

Throughout the twentieth century, even God's own Church failed to grasp the fullness of what God told Moses.

Throughout the 1800's and into the early 1900's, God's Church was losing His truth. The Church suffered mightily as the proliferation of churches, calling themselves Christian, was exploding on the world scene. This growing movement of new churches, with diverse faiths, held to the false doctrine of the Trinity. All of this had a strong adverse affect on God's people. This period of time was during the church era known as Sardis (Rev. 3:1-6). The era of Philadelphia followed and was led by God's end-time apostle and prophetic end-time Elijah, Herbert W. Armstrong.

God used Mr. Armstrong to restore truth to His Church since it had been dying out during the era of Sardis. In order to restore truth to the Church, God revealed what was true to Mr. Armstrong. God led him to understand that the Trinity was a false doctrine of the Catholic Church. He learned that the holy spirit was not a spirit being, but the power of God.

Although Mr. Armstrong understood that the Trinity was a lie, God did not give him full understanding of what was true concerning Himself and His Son, Jesus Christ. God did not fully lead him out from the pollution of the false Trinity doctrine. Mr. Armstrong still believed that Jesus Christ had eternally existed. God gave Mr. Armstrong enough to conclude that the Trinity was a lie, but He did not lead him fully into the truth. God reserved this revelation until now, at this very end time, during the time of the opening and the fulfillment of the Sixth Seal of Revelation.

The primary reason God reserved the fullness of this knowledge, until now, is to reveal who is His end-time prophet. Those whom God awakens from spiritual sleep, who have been scattered in His Church, will come to see the fullness of what He is revealing; and as a consequence, they will also recognize that I am who I say I am—God's end-time prophet and the spokesman of the two end-time witnesses.

Mr. Armstrong could only **see** what God revealed for him to see. Only God can reveal His truth to others, and no one can know that truth unless God gives it. God did not give everything about Himself to Mr. Armstrong in regard to the false teaching of the Trinity. This in no way detracts from Mr. Armstrong being God's end-time apostle and prophetic end-time Elijah.

One of the most profound things that God did reveal to Mr. Armstrong concerning Himself and His plan for mankind was that God is planning a family—a God Family. The God Family is referred to in different ways in scripture. One is the Kingdom of God, and another is the very name of His Family—**Elohim**.

Elohim is a uniplural Hebrew word. It is most often translated simply as "God" in English. But there are other Hebrew words that are also translated as God. Words have great meaning when they are understood for what they truly convey. However, much has been hidden because translations have been interpreted by people who did not know God and did not know His plan and purpose for mankind.

Again, God's purpose for mankind is that, in God's time, people will be given opportunity to become part of the God-kind, members of God's Family. As a reminder, when the 144,000 are resurrected, they will be the first of those born from among mankind to become a part of God's Family. They will be changed into immortal spirit beings, God beings, just like their elder brother Jesus Christ.

Since Mr. Armstrong was given understanding of Elohim being the name of the God Family and that God's purpose was for mankind to become part of His Family, then this revealed more fully the lie of the closed triune Godhead in the fable of the Trinity.

However, the truth in all this is that there is only one God who has eternally existed and His name is Yahweh—the Eternal One, the Self-Existing One. Look at what God told the Israelites:

> *I am the ETERNAL ONE [Yahweh], and there is **no one*** ***else**, there is no God [Elohim] except me. I strengthened you, although you have not known me, so that they may know from the rising of the sun, and from the west, that there is **no one except me**. I am the ETERNAL ONE [Yahweh], and there is **no one else**. (Is. 45:5-6)*

Elohim is the name of the God Family. It is similar to a family name like "Jones" or "Smith." Mankind has many family names, but the God kind will have only one family name—Elohim. God Almighty (El Shaddai), who spoke to Abraham, revealed Himself more fully to Moses by saying that His name was Yahweh Elohim.

The Truth About Yahweh

God's end-time apostle, Mr. Herbert W. Armstrong, was given understanding that the Trinity was a false teaching. He learned that the holy spirit is not a being, but that it is the very power of God. He also learned that God's purpose for mankind is for them to become members of the God Family (Elohim) and that God's Family is not a closed trinity, but instead, it can grow into the billions.

But there is only one eternally-existing member of Elohim and that is the ETERNAL ONE (Yahweh).

Mr. Armstrong was never able to come to understand this about God. He was not completely able to break free from the pollution of the Trinity doctrine because he believed that Jesus Christ was the God of the Old Testament. God never revealed to him the entire truth of the matter. No one on earth understands the true depth of this matter.

There is a quote regarding this subject in an article written by Mr. Armstrong, *Is Jesus God?*:

> Yes, Jesus is "Jehovah," although this word is a mistranslation used in the American Standard Version. The original name, in the Hebrew, contained the consonants "YHVH." In writing in Hebrew, vowels were omitted, supplied only in speaking. Thus the precise pronunciation of the name is not definitely known, but today it is commonly assumed to be Yahveh, or Yahweh. The meaning, in English, is "The Eternal," or "The Everliving," or the "Self-Existent." It commonly supposed that Yahveh, or, as commonly called, "Jehovah", or, as in the Authorized Version, "The LORD," of the Old Testament was God the FATHER of Jesus Christ. This is a flagrant error!

Mr. Armstrong fully believed that the Yahweh of the Old Testament writings was Jesus Christ, who would later divest Himself of His Godly power in order to be born human of His mother, Mary. However, this is not the case. The full story of the birth of Jesus Christ and the understanding of how such a thing came to be is a most awesome story indeed.

Scriptures quoted in the New Testament from Old Testament writings clarify that the Father of Jesus Christ was Yahweh (the ETERNAL ONE). One such area of scripture is in Acts 2 on the day of Pentecost when the holy spirit had been poured out upon the apostles. Peter was inspired to quote some of the Psalms that had been written by King David. Peter was showing the Jews that these verses were not about David, as the Jews supposed, but they were about Jesus Christ and God His Father.

In order to clarify what Peter is quoting, the scriptures will be placed side by side for easier comparison. The bracketed [ ] areas are inserted for explanation.

(Acts 2:25-28) *For David spoke concerning him* [Jesus Christ], *I* [Christ] *fore-saw the* **LORD** **[Yahweh]** *always before my* [Christ] *face, for* **He** *is on my* [Christ] *right hand, that I should not be moved: 26 Therefore did my* [Christ] *heart rejoice, and my* [Christ] *tongue was glad; moreover also my* [Jesus Christ] *flesh shall rest in hope: 27 Because* **you** *wilt not leave my* [Christ] *soul in hell* [Gk.–"hades" meaning the grave], *neither wilt* **you** *allow* **your** *Holy One* [Christ] *to see corruption* [decay of the body after death]. *28* **You** *have made known to me* [Jesus Christ] *the ways of life;* **you** *shall make me* [Christ] *full of joy with* **your** *countenance.*

(Ps. 16:8-11) *I* [Jesus Christ] *have set the* **ETERNAL ONE** **[Heb.--Yahweh]** *always before me because* **He** *is at my* [Jesus Christ] *right hand and I* [Jesus Christ] *shall not be moved. 9 Therefore my* [Jesus Christ] *heart is glad, and my* [Jesus Christ] *glory rejoices, and my* [Jesus Christ] *flesh also shall rest in hope. 10 For* **you** *wilt not leave my* [Jesus Christ] *soul in hell* [Heb.–"sheol" meaning the grave]; *neither will* **you** *allow* **your** *Holy One to see corruption* [destruction of the flesh]. *11* **You** *will show me the path of life, and in* **your** *presence is fullness of joy, and at* **your** *right hand there are pleasures for evermore.*

Peter continues by saying that what is written by David is not about him [David] because he is still dead and in his grave.

<u>Acts 2:29-31</u> *Men and brethren, let me freely speak unto you of the patriarch David, that he is both dead and buried, and his sepulcher is with us unto this day. 30 Therefore being a prophet* [David], *and knowing that* **God** [**Yahweh**] *had sworn to him* [David] *with an oath, that of the fruit of his* [David's] *loins, according to the flesh,* **HE** *would raise up* <u>Christ</u> [the Messiah] *to sit on his* [David's] *throne. 31 He* [David] *seeing this before spoke of the resurrection of Christ, that* <u>his</u> *soul* [Christ's] *was not left in hell* [the grave], *neither his flesh did see corruption.*

<u>Acts 2:32-36</u> *This* <u>Jesus</u> *has* **God** *raised up, whereof we all are witnesses. 33 Therefore being by the right hand of* **God** *exalted, and having received of the* **Father** *the promise of the holy spirit,* **He** *has shed forth this, which you now see and hear. 34 For David is not ascended into the heavens: but he* [David] *himself said, The* **LORD** [**Yahweh**] *said to my* [David's] <u>Lord</u>*, Sit thou on* **My** *right hand, 35 Until I make* <u>your</u> [Christ's] *foes* <u>your</u> [Christ's] *footstool. 36 Therefore let all the house of Israel know assuredly, that* **God** *has made this same* <u>Jesus</u>*, whom you have crucified, both* <u>Lord</u> *and* <u>Christ</u>*.*

[Since David was a prophet, he knew what the ETERNAL had promised concerning the Messiah who would be born of his lineage and would one day sit upon his (David's) throne (over Israel). {quote in Psalms 132:11}]

(Psalm 110:1) *The* **ETERNAL** [**Heb.–Yahweh**] *said to my* [David's] <u>Lord</u> [Christ], *Sit* <u>you</u> [Christ] *at* **my** [Yahweh's] *right hand, until* **I** *make* <u>your</u> *enemies* <u>your</u> *footstool.*

In the scriptures that we have covered so far, God Almighty [El Shaddai] revealed Himself to Abraham, Isaac and Jacob. When He called Moses to lead the children of Israel out of Egypt, He revealed that His name was the ETERNAL God [Yahweh Elohim]. The ETERNAL God told Israel (Isaiah 45) that He was the only one who was God [Elohim]. In other words, He was the only one of the God Family at this time. There was no one else!

Certainly the teaching of the Trinity is a lie! In addition, Jesus Christ was not the ETERNAL [Yahweh] of the Old Testament. Indeed, Jesus Christ has not eternally existed. If anyone believes differently, there are scriptures that can be misinterpreted if you read other ideas into them, just as traditional Christianity has done.

Peter explained the verses he quoted from the Psalms (Acts 2:32-36), and he makes it clear that God raised up Jesus Christ from the dead. Jesus Christ was dead when He was in the tomb. He had no life in Him. He was not eternal! God, His Father, had to raise Him from the dead.

The ETERNAL is Christ's Father

The Bible is quite clear about the fact that the ETERNAL [Yahweh] God [Elohim] is the Father of Jesus Christ. Jesus Christ was begotten directly of the Father, and He (Jesus) had no life until His beginning when He was born of His mother Mary.

Let's look at other areas that describe this relationship between the ETERNAL God and His Son, Jesus Christ:

> *The **God** of our fathers raised up Jesus, whom you laid hands on to kill and hanged on a tree. Him has **God** exalted with his right hand to be a Prince and a Savior, for to give repentance to Israel, and forgiveness of sins.* (Acts 5:30-31)

The "God of our fathers" is an expression that always refers to the ETERNAL [Yahweh], just as He introduced Himself to Moses by explaining that He was the God of Abraham, Isaac and Jacob—the God of our fathers. Peter explained here that it was this same God who exalted Jesus Christ by placing Him at His (God's) right hand, and by making Him (Christ) a Prince and a Savior of mankind through the forgiveness of sins (as our Passover):

> The **God** of Abraham, Isaac and Jacob, the **God** of our fathers, has glorified **His** Son Jesus, whom you delivered up, and denied him in the presence of Pilate when he was determined to let him go. But you denied the Holy One and the Just, and desired a murderer to be granted to you. You killed the Prince of life, whom **God** has raised from the dead, whereof we are witnesses. (Acts 3:13-15)

In these verses, Peter is clearly stating that Jesus Christ is the Son of the God of our fathers: Abraham, Isaac and Jacob.

Jesus Christ, in His own words, makes it clear who His Father is. He too quoted one of the verses that Peter used when explaining some of the same things:

> While the Pharisees were gathered together, Jesus asked them, saying, "What do you think of Christ [the Messiah]? **Whose son is he?**" Then they said to him, "The Son of David." He said to them, "How is it then that David in spirit [for David was a prophet] calls him Lord, saying, 'The **LORD** [the ETERNAL—Yahweh] said unto my [David's] Lord, "Sit thou on my right hand, till I make your enemies your footstool?"' If David then calls him Lord, how is he his [David's] son?" And no man was able to answer him a word, neither dared any man from that day forth ask him any more questions. (Matthew 22:41-46)

The whole point that Jesus Christ was making to the Pharisees was that David (as a prophet inspired in the spirit) wrote in the Psalms that the coming Messiah was his Lord. Therefore the Messiah could not be the son of David. Only the ETERNAL could be His (the Messiah's) Father.

The apostle Paul also quoted from the Old Testament writings to make it clear that Jesus Christ is the Son of God and that Christ is now God—in the God Family:

> *God* [the only God known to the Israelites—Yahweh], *who at different times and in many ways spoke in time past to the fathers through the prophets, has in these last days spoken to us through His Son, whom He has appointed heir of all things, through whom also He made the worlds* [ages to come]. [It is through Jesus Christ that God will fulfill His plan for mankind.] *Who being the brightness of His* [God's] *glory, and the express image of His substance, and upholding all things by the word of His power, when He* [Jesus Christ] *had by Himself purged our sins, sat down on the right hand of the Majesty on high. Who being made so much better than the angels, as He has by inheritance obtained a more excellent name than them. For to which of the angels did He say at any time, "You are My Son, this day have I begotten you?" And again, "I will be to him a Father, and He shall be to Me a Son?" And again, when He brings in the first begotten into the world, He* [God] *said, "And let all the angels of God worship him* [Jesus Christ].*" And of the angels He says, "Who makes His angels spirit, and His ministers a flame of fire* [the angels were made spirit beings, but Jesus Christ was made God].*" But to the Son He says, "Your throne, O God,*

is for ever and ever: a scepter of righteousness is the scepter of your kingdom." (Hebrews 1:1-8)

There are so many scriptures that make it clear the ETERNAL ONE (Yahweh) is the Father of Jesus Christ that it is difficult to imagine anyone could believe otherwise.

In one last example, Paul again is very specific concerning what he is saying about this matter even as he quotes the very scripture he is explaining:

*But **God** raised him [Paul was speaking of Christ] from the dead. Then He was seen for many days by those who came up with Him from Galilee to Jerusalem, who are His witnesses to the people. And we are declaring to you this good news [Gk.– gospel], how that the promise which was made to the fathers, God has fulfilled the same unto us their children in that **He** has raised up Jesus again, as it is also written in the second psalm, "You [Christ] are **My** [Yahweh] Son, this day have I begotten you."* (Acts 13:30-33)

Notice the scripture Paul quoted:

*"Yet have **I** set **My** king upon **My** holy hill of Zion. I will declare the decree," the **ETERNAL ONE** [Yahweh] has said to me [Christ], "You are My Son; this day have I begotten you."* (Psalm 2:6-7)

The WORD Made Flesh

As you begin to understand the very means by which God accomplished all that He did through His Son, Jesus Christ, you may then begin to understand more clearly the very means by which mankind can begin to change (be transformed) to become like God, becoming of the same mind with Him—at one, in agreement with Him. It is what is in our minds that makes us who we are, and our identity has everything to do with the very thoughts that proceed from us (reflecting the way we think).

Knowing who the ETERNAL God is in scripture is far from **knowing** the ETERNAL God. This is something that traditional Christianity has never come to grasp, especially concerning Jesus Christ. They believe they "know" Him and will often ask others if they "know" Jesus Christ. They speak in terms of what they have learned in their churches about the story of Jesus Christ and how He died for our sins. They like the stories that have evolved in their faith (through the doctrines of their particular church teachings), but they do not **know** Jesus Christ.

To truly know the ETERNAL God and Jesus Christ is to believe what they said because what they have said reflects the very thoughts of their mind, of **the way they are**! If people cannot accept something as simple as what God and Jesus Christ say about the weekly seventh-day Sabbath, then they cannot come to know God's purpose that is revealed through it. They cannot come to know God! If people refuse what God and Jesus Christ have to say about Passover, then they will never be able to come to understand God's great purpose He is accomplishing through the Passover.

Since traditional Christianity refuses to observe the Passover, as God and Jesus Christ command, then it cannot come to truly **know** them. Judaism will not observe the Passover as God commands, and therefore, it does not know God, since all of God's plan for mankind begins with the revelation that He gives through the Passover.

Jesus Christ made a statement that people do not understand. They do not grasp how profound His statement was. It sounds like a nice platitude to many, but they simply do not "get it:"

Jesus answered him by saying, "It is written that man shall not live by bread alone, but by every word of God." (Luke 4:4)

Most of the things God has told man are about the very things that lead to eternal life in His Family. If you truly desire to have the eternal life God can give, which is beyond this physical life that is sustained by the food we eat, then you must eat (spiritually) of what God gives you through His word. You must eat of the very word of God that reflects the mind, purpose and ways of God. People must come to embrace the **true word** of God (not the interpretations of traditional Christianity) if they really want to know God and have a right relationship with Him and His Son.

There were many times when Jesus explained things about Himself that God was giving to mankind, but people did not understand. He said, *"He who comes from above is above all"* (John 3:31). Christ was speaking of Himself by explaining that He came out from His Father (begotten of Him) who is above in heaven, and that because of this, He (Jesus Christ) was above all. He explained more:

> *He who is of the earth is earthly* [physical], *and speaks of the earth* [of physical things]. *He who comes from heaven is above all, and He testifies of what He has seen and heard* [spiritually]. (John 3:31-32)

Jesus explained that He was from above, from His Father, and that all He spoke (gave testimony) was fully from God. He added:

> *For He whom God has sent speaks the words of God because God does not give the spirit to Him by measure.* (John 3:34)

Jesus Christ was not limited in the power of God to know Him or to be fully at one with Him through the spirit.

This powerful relationship between the Father and the Son was accomplished through the very means by which Jesus Christ came to be the Son of God.

"In the beginning was the Word, and the Word was <u>*with*</u> [Gk.– unto] *God, and the* **Word** *was* **God**" (John 1:1). When it states that the Word was "with" God, the Greek means that the "Word was unto God," which is saying that the Word was God's and it was unto no other. There are other words in Greek that convey "being with" someone or "beside someone," but this word "unto" means that it is fully "unto" (belonging to) the one being spoken of, exclusively so.

"The same was in the beginning <u>*with*</u> [Gk.– unto] *God"* (John 1:2). John introduces the beginning of the life of Jesus Christ that came from the Father. He did this by focusing on the Word. In Greek, the "Word" is Logos and means "the revelatory thought." It is the essence that identifies one's very thoughts, thinking and identity. Indeed, there has never been a time without God and all that identifies who He is. As with every individual, we are identified by that which we think in the mind and also in the very thoughts of the mind, which come out of an individual in actions. These actions reflect the "logos"—the revelatory thoughts.

The Word was unto God, and to no other, because there was no other. Everything that can be explained to man began from the Word who is God. From the Word, from God, His revelatory thought began to become manifest as He created the spirit world and the angelic realm. Later, He created the physical universe and eventually mankind. To this day, He continues to reveal His will in all that He has purposed. This is God. This is the Word of God being made manifest (revealed) to the world. Indeed:

All things were made by <u>Him</u> [referring to the Word who is God], *and without <u>Him</u>* [again, the Word who is God] *nothing was made that was made. In <u>him</u>* [the Word who is God] *was life, and the life was the light of men.* (John 1:3-4)

All that exists comes from the planning and purpose of God, which He formulated and determined. This is summed up in the Word of God and is a matter of the very **will** of God.

God's plan is to share His understanding, His wisdom, His very Word with mankind: so that we can all come into unity of spirit with the same purpose—with the same will. We are to be individually unique, but we are also to **be at one** (complete unity of spirit) with the very will, mind, purpose, and way of God.

The **way** to such life was first made manifest in Jesus Christ. It is through Jesus Christ that we are shown how such life, in unity of spirit, is possible in the God Family (in Elohim). However, as this book has described, the transformation (change), from physical, carnal nature to spirit, Godly nature, is not an easy process for mankind.

From the beginning, before anything else was, there was only Yahweh El Elohim, the ETERNAL God of the God Family. Then the time came for the next member (the second member). He would be the first to be begotten and later to be born as the first of the firstfruits to enter the God Family (Elohim). The time in God's plan came for the Passover to come to mankind, later to be resurrected as Jesus Christ Elohim—Jesus Christ of the God Family.

Speaking of Jesus Christ, John went on to say:

Then the Word was made flesh, and dwelt among us, (and we beheld His glory, the glory as of the only begotten of the Father,) full of grace and truth. (John 1:14)

The very revelatory thought (Word, Logos) of God Almighty was given to Jesus Christ, in Jesus Christ, and was the very manifestation, **the revelation of God to man**. Jesus Christ was born with the very mind of God, who was His Father, but He grew up separately with His own identity being formed through all that He experienced in His physical life, having His own individuality that was unique, and apart from His Father.

John later records something that is even far more profound that God was revealing to mankind, which mankind had never received before.

God IN Christ

In John 14, Jesus Christ told the disciples that since they believed God, they also were to believe Him. Believing in Christ is far beyond simply believing that He lived and died nearly 2,000 years ago for the sins of mankind. Instead, it has everything to do with **believing all that He said**, which the world does not.

Jesus told them it was now time for Him to go and prepare a place for them. People do not grasp what He was telling them. He gave them these words on the very last night of His physical life on earth, on the night of the Passover. The time had come for Him to die as the Passover for all mankind and then be resurrected from the dead, as the first to enter Elohim, the God Family, the Kingdom of God. As Jesus Christ Elohim, He could now complete more of God's plan by making the way for others who would also enter the Family.

Jesus told the disciples, *"Where I go you know, and the **way** you know"* (John 14:4). Then, Thomas responded by saying that they did not know where He was going, so how could they know the way. Jesus Christ was not talking about a location, but a **way** of life to be lived that would lead into being in the God Family.

So Jesus responded by saying, *"I am **the way**, the truth and the life, and no man comes to the Father except by* [through] *me"* (John 14:6).

God was revealing that the way into His Family and the way of becoming at one with Him, in unity of spirit, was through His Son, Jesus Christ. The very process that was at work in Jesus Christ was about to begin working in others, in order to accomplish a transformation of the mind, which would lead into God's Family. The process of change that is to take place in mankind is through the process of repentance and turning to God's way of life. But man cannot accomplish this by his own efforts or will power. It requires the power of God that can work in the mind to change the way we think so that we come into unity and agreement with God. It is interesting to note that the word which is translated as "repent" in scripture, actually means "to think differently" in the Greek.

Now, Jesus Christ was going to reveal even more to the disciples to show how this process would be accomplished:

> *If you had known Me, you should have known my Father also, and from this time you have **known** Him, and have seen Him.* (John 14:7)

This saying was confusing to the disciples, so Philip responded by saying that if Christ would simply show them the Father then that would satisfy their understanding. But Jesus was speaking of something spiritual, not physical. The disciples were limited in their thinking to that which is physical:

> *Have I been such a long time with you, and yet you have not known Me Philip? He who has seen Me has seen the Father, so how do you say then, "Show us the Father?"* (John 14:9)

Again, this is similar to the expressions people use when talking about "believing in Jesus Christ," but traditional Christianity fails to grasp that such a thing means much more concerning Christ. It is a matter of **knowing** His mind, His very being that is summed up in the "Word," which is from God the Father, and this reveals God's true way of life. Notice what Christ went on to say:

> *Don't you believe that I am in* [a spiritual reality] *the Father, and the Father is in me? The words that I speak to you, I do not speak from myself, but the Father who dwells in me, He does the works.* (John 14:10)

Jesus Christ took no credit for Himself, and He was revealing that He was of the exact same mind and in full agreement with the Father. He was showing that this was being accomplished by God the Father **dwelling in** Him through the power of the spirit, which conveys (communicates) the Word, the very mind of God, to whom He (God) will. Christ was showing that He (Jesus) was in full unity with the Father, with the Word of God, and so those things that came through Him were fully from God:

> *Believe me that I am in the Father, and the Father is in me, or else believe me for the very works' sake.* (John 14:11)

He told them that if they could not believe Him when He said that the Father was **in** Him and He was **in** the Father, then they should at least believe Him because of all the works they had witnessed, which could only be from God.

Jesus Christ went through this discourse with the disciples so that they (and any who would listen) could begin to understand that God was beginning to work in mankind to enable him to experience understanding and growth on a spiritual plane. In time, this is the very process that will lead into becoming part of the God Family.

God and Christ IN Man

By telling the disciples these things, Jesus Christ was preparing them for the coming of the holy spirit that would be poured out upon them, beginning on the day of Pentecost. Through His dying, as the payment for the sins of all mankind, He fulfilled the purpose God revealed through the Passover Lamb. After His resurrection, Jesus Christ became our High Priest, and through Him, man could now have access to the very throne of God.

Having access to God has been made possible because sin can be forgiven through Jesus Christ. God will not be in the presence of sin, and therefore, will not **dwell in** those who are not being forgiven of sin. The reason Jesus Christ died is so that we could be forgiven through Him and so that God the Father and Jesus Christ could **dwell in** mankind. This is the only means whereby the holy spirit of God can dwell **in** us, so that we can be transformed (in our thinking) in order to come into unity and oneness with God's true way of life.

In regard to what would happen on Pentecost and continue on within the Church, Jesus Christ told the disciples the importance of the holy spirit that would be sent to them. He had been their advocate, the one who, up until now, had been with them to give them aid and help in God's way of life; but now He was going to die, so He told them that He would now pray to His Father to send them another advocate:

> *I will pray to the Father, and He will give you another advocate* [Gk.–helper, one who gives aid], *that he may* **abide** *with you for ever.* (John 14:16)

This word for "advocate" in the Greek has confused some scholars because it is a masculine word, like many other inanimate objects. "Advocate," in this case, is not a being as some have supposed. Jesus Christ is referred to as our advocate in

1 John 2:1, but in this case, Jesus Christ is referring to the holy spirit that would be poured out upon them to give them help and aid. Since Christ was no longer going to be with them (in their physical presence), they needed the advocate that was the holy spirit. Receiving the holy spirit in their lives meant that God the Father and Jesus Christ would be with them and literally **in** them, through the spirit that can **dwell in** the mind, **in** the spirit essence that is already in man.

Christ explained about the advocate:

> *The Spirit of truth which the world cannot receive because it sees it not, neither knows it. But you know it because it dwells with you, and shall be **in** you.* (John 14:17)

The holy spirit is something that cannot be received or experienced by people in the world until God gives it after He grants them repentance and forgiveness. So the world cannot **know** the things that only the spirit of God can convey to the human mind. The spirit of God gives mankind the ability to see (understand, know) things of the spirit—of God and His true ways.

God revealed a most incredible thing to the disciples, but people have not understood what Christ was saying:

> *I will not leave you guideless. I __will come__* [Gk.–"am coming"] *to you.* (John 14:18)

This is the same expression that He used in a previous verse:

> *If I go and prepare a place for you, I __will come__ again, and receive you to Myself, so that where I am, there you may be also.* (John 14:3)

Jesus Christ **is not speaking** of a future event concerning His eventual return at His second coming, since this word that is translated "will come" is not a future tense verb. In the Greek, it is "present tense, indicative mood, middle voice." Since English does not have a middle voice, it is usually difficult to translate the middle voice into English. A way to better understand what is being said is to understand the "present progressive tense" in English grammar.

This would be most difficult for a translator who does not understand God and the way He is going to help bring about a complete transformation in the mind of man from a carnal, selfish spirit to a giving, completely unselfish spirit.

The peculiar tense of this word determines a very special meaning. It means that, at some point, Jesus Christ will begin coming and He will continue to come. This has no meaning if you are speaking of physical human beings. But God was revealing that He and His Son would begin, at some point, to come into a person's life through the power of the holy spirit and that they would continue to do so, abiding in (dwelling in, living in) the individual. This is why Jesus continued with His explanation of the holy spirit which would be given, as an advocate, after He was in heaven:

> *Yet a little while, and the world sees me no more, but you will see me, and because I live, you will live also. At that day you will know that I am **in** My Father, and you **in** Me, and **I** in you.* (John 14:19-20)

He explained that the world would no longer be able to see Him (physically) because He was about to be killed, entombed and then resurrected into heaven. He explained that the disciples would be able to see Him (spiritually) and that because He would live, they would live also (spiritually).

Christ said that when the holy spirit began to come to them (the disciples) that this would be the time that they could know (spiritually experience) that the Father and Christ were **dwelling**

in them, and they (the disciples) **in** Them. On Pentecost this process began, God the Father and Jesus Christ began to come into the lives (minds) of the disciples (spiritually) and to **dwell in** them. As others would be called into the Church (be baptized, and receive the impregnation of the holy spirit—begotten spiritually), then they, too, would begin to experience this same life **dwelling in** them (continually coming into them).

On Pentecost, God began **dwelling in** mankind. This is the very thing that Jesus Christ was revealing to His disciples on His last night of physical life, on the Passover night. This is one of the most profound things that God has ever revealed to mankind—how He and His Son could dwell **in** man and **continue doing so** in order to bring about a spiritual transformation in man's spirit. It wasn't until this point, after 4,000 years of man on earth, that God revealed this to a select few; and it is now nearly 2,000 years beyond that time that God has chosen to begin the process of revealing these things to all mankind:

> *He who has my commandments, and keeps them is he who loves Me* [to truly come to know God is to live by the way of life contained in His words—in His commandments]. *He who loves Me will be loved of My Father, and I will love him, and I will* manifest [to reveal spiritually, to make Himself known] *Myself to him. Judas said to Him, not Iscariot, "Lord, how is it that you will manifest Yourself to us and not to the world?" Jesus answered and said to him, "If a man love me he will keep my words, and my Father will love him, and we **will come** to him, and make our **abode** [Gk.– dwelling place] with him. He who does not love Me does not keep My* word

[logos], *and the <u>word</u>* [logos] *which you hear is not Mine, but the Father's who sent Me."* (John 14:21-24)

When Jesus Christ said that He and His Father would come into the disciples' lives and make their <u>abode</u> [**Gk.– dwelling place**] with them, He was explaining something more fully which He had already introduced to them:

*In My <u>Father's house</u> are many **mansions**. If it were not so, I would have told you. I go to prepare a place for you.* (John 14:2)

The word that is translated as "mansions" is so often translated incorrectly. This word is used in only one other place and that is in verse 23 where it is correctly translated as "abode," which in the Greek means a "dwelling place."

Yes, God's plan includes His ability to make His dwelling in us possible by the holy spirit that He gives once a person has been baptized and begotten of God's spirit. After that, God will dwell in us and continue doing so, as long as we are faithful to continue the process of repentance and seeking His life to remain in us.

The apostle Paul explained this same process in Ephesians:

For through Him [Jesus Christ] *we both have access by one Spirit unto the Father. Therefore you are now no longer strangers and foreigners, but fellow citizens with the saints* [of those God has called], *and of the **household** of God.* (Ephesians 2:18-19)

This is the very thing Christ was speaking of when He said, "In My Father's house are many dwelling places (places of abode)." In other words, the household of God is made of many who will be able to become part of the God Family, in the Temple of God (spiritual), in the Household of God:

You are being built upon the foundation of the apostles
and prophets, with Jesus Christ Himself being the chief
corner stone. **In whom** *all the building, fitly framed*
together, grows into a <u>*holy temple*</u> **in the Lord.**
(Ephesians 2:20-21)

God is revealing here that once people are called into a
relationship with Him and are baptized and receive the
impregnation of the holy spirit, then they become a part of a
spiritual household—the spiritual Temple of God. Through
God dwelling in man, man can begin the process of
transformation:

In whom *you also are being built together for a*
habitation [place to dwell] *of God through the spirit.*
(Ephesians 2:22)

There is much more to learn about this process, but this has
shown the purpose and means by which God was able to **dwell** <u>**in**</u>
His own Son in order to fulfill His purpose for mankind through
Jesus Christ being our Passover. It is through all that Jesus Christ
fulfilled as our Passover, and then being resurrected as our High
Priest, that now God also can dwell in mankind to bring about the
complete change which is necessary in order to be born into the
very Family of God—Elohim!

It is through the means of God dwelling in mankind that the
mind can be changed from selfish to unselfish, from the way of
get to the way of give, and from carnal (physical) thinking to
Godly (spiritual) thinking. This is what Paul explained:

Do not be conformed to this world [to the ways of this
world, which is natural], *but be you* <u>*transformed*</u> *by the*
renewing of your mind, *so that you may prove what is*
that good, and acceptable, and perfect, will of God.
(Romans 12:2)

It is only by having God's life (the holy spirit) dwelling in us that we can have our thinking (minds) changed to come into unity and oneness with the will and word of God. Our minds must be renewed, and it is by this means that we can begin to prove God's way. We then can begin to put His ways into action in our lives, so that we can prove to ourselves that only God's way of life is good and perfect.

Hopefully the following scripture that God said through Paul will now mean more to you, *"Let this mind be in you, which was also in Christ Jesus"* (Philippians 2:5). The very mind of God, the Word (Logos), was made flesh. Jesus Christ became the Word of God that was made manifest to mankind. God's purpose is that this same mind dwell in man, to transform him, so he can eventually enter His (God's) very family, the Family of God, the Kingdom of God—Elohim.

Made in the Image of God

God is reproducing Himself by building a Family that will become the Kingdom of God. This has been God's plan and purpose from the very beginning, before anything was ever created, including the spirit world with the angelic realm. Before God created anything, He determined how He would fulfill His plan. God predetermined that man would be made in His very image, after His likeness. This first phase was the physical phase of His creation of mankind when He (God) made his (man's) physical appearance after His image.

The spiritual creation of how God is working with mankind has been covered, in part, in the previous section. This phase of God's creation is to make man after His likeness, on a spiritual plane, by transforming the very mind of man, so that man can come into unity and oneness with God, His Word and His way of life.

This transformation of mankind is accomplished by being able to be begotten spiritually, just as a child is begotten in its mother's womb and later born into the world. After being spiritually begotten by God, He (God) and His Son are able to dwell in the one who has been begotten. It is by this process of being begotten and being in the womb (in the Church who is the mother of us all) that a spiritual creation begins. This spiritual creation continues in spiritual growth until the time it can be born (of spirit) into the Kingdom of God, into the Family of God, becoming Elohim. Indeed, mankind has been made in the image of God (on a physical plane), but once begotten, a transformation takes place in the mind until one can be born into the very likeness of God (on a spiritual plane) after becoming spirit and in the God Family.

There is so much more that could be written concerning these things about God's great plan, but only two more areas will be covered in this book. If anyone has a genuine desire to learn more, then they can go to a website where many of my sermons are posted (www.cog-pkg.org). Some of the things addressed in this chapter are covered more fully in a series of sermons (lectures) that can be found in the section entitled the "Feast of Tabernacles—2005."

From the very beginning when God created mankind, He began to reveal His purpose for doing so:

> *For thus says the ETERNAL ONE* [Yahweh] *who created the heavens, God* [Elohim] *Himself who formed the earth and made it, He who has established it, He who created it not in vain* [Heb.–"tohoo" – in confusion, without form], *but who formed it to be inhabited, "I am the ETERNAL ONE* [Yahweh], *and there is no one else."* (Is. 45:18)

As covered in a previous chapter, the ETERNAL God created the earth in great beauty, but Satan later rebelled, along with a third of the angelic realm, and in time set out to destroy what God had created. Their attempt to destroy the creation led to a type of nuclear winter that engulfed the earth. When we come on the scene in the beginning of Genesis, we **are not** reading about the original creation of the universe, our solar system and the earth; but we are reading about the earth being refashioned so that it could be inhabited with life once more:

> *In the beginning God* **[Elohim]** *created the heaven and the earth.* [this refers to the very beginning when the heavens and earth were first created] *And the earth became without form, and void* [remember that God said He had not created it this way, but it became this way because of Satan's rebellion], *and darkness was upon the face of the deep. Then the spirit of God* **[Elohim]** *moved upon the face of the waters. God* **[Elohim]** *said, "Let there be light, and there was light." God* **[Elohim]** *saw the light that it was good, and God* **[Elohim]** *separated the light from the darkness* [He established the cycle of the day once again]. *And God* **[Elohim]** *called the light day, and the darkness he called night. Then the evening and the morning were the first day.* (Genesis 1:1-5)

So God began his remolding of the earth by placing it in its perfect orbit and rotation once again. God established the first day by beginning with the sunset of one day, which is at the beginning of night, and continuing through the daylight portion to the next sunset. Biblically this is God's pattern for one complete day. That is why the seventh-day Sabbath actually begins at sundown of the sixth day and is complete at sundown at the end of the seventh day.

Then God created mankind:

And God [**Elohim**] *said, "Let us make man in our image, after our likeness, and let them have dominion over the fish of the sea, and over the fowl of the air, and over the cattle, and over all the earth, and over every moving thing that moves upon the earth."* (Gen. 1:26)

It has been confusing to some that God said, "Let us make man in our image, after our likeness." Some have believed He was referring to the angels who assisted Him, but this is wrong. Some have believed He was speaking to another member of the God Family, but this is wrong.

God revealed His plan and purpose by inspiring these verses in Genesis 1 to use only the word Elohim. God did this for great reason because He was showing the purpose of all that He worked to do during those first six days, and on this sixth day He created mankind. The word Elohim is used to show His purpose because the word is a uniplural word that reveals His Family and the name He has given it—Elohim. It was Yahweh Elohim who created mankind, and He was speaking prophetically of His purpose for mankind to eventually be able to be in Elohim. Man was not only being created to have a physical appearance with a likeness to God, but eventually he was to be able to be fully created in the spiritual image and likeness of God. Man was to be begotten of the spirit and grow in it until born of spirit into the God Family.

This is an awkward translation in Genesis 1:26, and it is far from correct. The words for image and likeness refer to the word Elohim. It is simply saying, "Let man be made in the same image and after the same likeness of Elohim." The creation of man was not the complete creation that God purposed (preordained, predetermined) for mankind, but the physical creation was the beginning. The spiritual creation would come later, and it would be worked out through God's plan that included the next 7,000 years, thereby accomplishing a prophetic fulfillment of the seven-day week:

> *So God* [**Elohim**] *created man in His image. In the image of God* [**Elohim**] *He created him, as male and female He created them.* (Genesis 1:27)

On the seventh day, God rested from His work of making the earth inhabitable once more. He had begun the first phase of creating His own Family (Elohim), which involved the creation of man on a physical plane, and in time, the spiritual creation would follow.

It was the **ETERNAL God** who created and brought forth life:

> *Then the heavens and the earth were finished, and all the host of them, and on the seventh day God* [Elohim] *ended His work which He had made, and He rested on the seventh day from all his work which He had made. So God* [Elohim] *blessed the seventh day, and sanctified it, because that in it He had rested from all His work which God* [Elohim] *created and made. This was the time when life was brought forth in the heavens and in the earth, when all* [all life] *was created, and it was the time in which the ETERNAL* [**Yahweh**] *God* [**Elohim**] *fashioned the earth and the heavens* [the first heavens of our atmosphere]. (Gen. 2:1-4)

It was the **ETERNAL God** (Yahweh Elohim) who created and brought forth man:

> *And the ETERNAL* [**Yahweh**] *God* [**Elohim**] *formed man of the dust of the ground, and breathed into his nostrils the breath of life, and man became a living being.* (Genesis 2:7)

Clearly, it was the ETERNAL (Yahweh) God (Elohim), and He alone, who created mankind.

The First to Enter Elohim

Jesus Christ was the first of all mankind to enter the God Family. From the beginning there was only the ETERNAL God (Yahweh Elohim). Jesus Christ, after His death, became the **first** of all mankind to be resurrected from the dead and enter the Family of God, thereby becoming Jesus Christ Elohim:

> *But now is Christ risen from the dead, and has become the firstfruits of them that slept.* (1 Corinthians 15:20)

Jesus Christ is referred to as the "first" of the firstfruits of God, as He is the first to be resurrected from the dead, becoming spirit in composition, and the first to enter the Kingdom of God (Elohim). God reveals that many will enter His Family, Elohim. The 144,000 are referred to as the firstfruits of God's Family, since they will be the **first** from among the families of mankind to be resurrected and become God (Elohim). Paul went on to explain that there is an order to those who are resurrected:

> *But every man in his own order: Christ the firstfruits* [first of the firstfruits], *and afterward they that are Christ's at his coming.* (1 Corinthians 15:23)

The resurrection of additional billions will come at a future time beyond this.

As covered earlier, the purpose of God was not complete when He created mankind as physical human beings, but His greater purpose was for a spiritual creation. After human beings are begotten of the holy spirit, they will then grow spiritually until the time when they will be resurrected into the spirit Family of God. The apostle James spoke of this very thing:

> *Of His* [God's] *own will, we were begotten of Him with the word* [Gk.–"logos"– revelatory thought of God] *of truth, that we should be a kind of firstfruits of His creation.* (James 1:18)

The creation being spoken of here is the processes of creation whereby we are begotten of God's spirit, and through time, transformed in mind to unity and oneness with God. Once we have fully matured, then we can be born into God's very spirit Family—born into Elohim.

Jesus Christ was the first to be born of the spiritual likeness and image of God, the first born into the God Family. No human being, born solely of mankind, could fulfill what Jesus Christ did in fulfilling the role of Passover of all mankind. The process required that Jesus Christ's Father be God Almighty. Jesus Christ could have one physical parent, His mother Mary, but His Father had to be God. Jesus Christ would have to be born with the very mind of God dwelling in Him—the Word made flesh. When He was born into the world, He was born fully individual, as any other child, except that His Father was God, and His mind was from God (not man); and this enabled Him to have full unity of purpose and will. There is much more to this process, but this is the first step for you to be able to understand.

Paul spoke of Jesus Christ, *"Who is the image of the invisible God, the firstborn of all creation"* (Colossians 1:15). Remember, God's purpose for mankind is that man be able to be born Elohim, as members of His Family. This is the purpose of all creation and Jesus Christ is spoken of here as the firstborn of all creation—the creation of bringing mankind into God's Family. **Everything** God created is about the ultimate purpose He is working out concerning the creation of His Family.

The very life that existed **in** Jesus from the beginning is the life that we can begin to have living **in** us (dwelling in us through the spirit) once we are begotten of God. Then, a new life begins to develop as our minds are transformed from physical selfishness to the ways of God. Now, we can share in that same life that dwelled **in** Christ, after we are forgiven of our sins and God begins to dwell **in** us after being begotten.

This has always been God's plan from the beginning, that mankind be able to be begotten of His spirit once our sins are atoned through the blood of Jesus Christ. From this point forward, we are to grow and be molded and fashioned into the very image and likeness of our elder brother Jesus Christ, so that we can be born into the God Family as He was:

> *For whom He* [Almighty God] *did foreknow, He also predetermined to be conformed to the image of His Son, that He might be the firstborn among many brethren.* (Romans 8:29)

Jesus Christ was the first to be born into God's Family. God planned from the beginning how mankind could also enter this Family in and through His Son. To understand Melchizedek is to more fully understand this process.

MELCHIZEDEK

People have speculated on the meaning of the story of Melchizedek, but no one has been able to really understand it. However, by learning the truth regarding this story, a person can actually begin to better understand how God worked in and through Jesus Christ for the purpose of accomplishing His will to create Elohim—the God Family.

How God Worked With Abraham

Much can be learned about how God can dwell **in** mankind by understanding how He revealed Himself to Abraham. Let's focus first upon the occasion when God and two angels visited Abraham. It was at this time that God first told Abraham that Sarah would give birth to a son, even though she was well beyond the years for childbearing. The entire story does not need to be repeated here, but only that portion that begins to reveal understanding:

> *The ETERNAL ONE* [Yahweh] *appeared to him* [Abraham] *in the plains of Mamre, as he* [Abraham] *sat in the tent door in the heat of the day. He lifted up his eyes and looked, and there before him were three men that stood out before him. When he saw them he ran from before the tent door to meet them, and bowed himself toward the ground, and said, "My Lord, if now I have found favor in your sight, do not continue on, but please stay here a while with your servant."* (Genesis 18:1-3)

The purpose in looking at these verses is to make several points. All three who appeared before Abraham appeared as physical men. Angelic beings are unable to appear to humans unless God grants them the ability to do so. When God reveals Himself through a physical manifestation (in the form of a human body), the conditions are unique. A physical body cannot contain Almighty God, but in some of His earlier encounters with man God did use a physical body through which to communicate.

It should be understood, as the Bible clearly teaches, that no one (no human) has ever seen God. When such a statement is made, it is speaking of the literal sense because mankind is incapable of seeing anything in the spirit world where God resides. Man cannot see spirit. Only when a physical manifestation (of that which is spirit) is given can man see something. This is not to be confused with those things Jesus Christ taught when He spoke of the ability to see the Father (John 14) and Himself (after His resurrection). In those examples, Christ was speaking of things that are of the spirit, which have to do with understanding (seeing spiritually) and the revelation of God (seeing the ways of God, mind of God, truth of God, and identity of God—to know God). When Jesus explained such things it never concerned a person's physical ability to see God.

There was an occasion when God revealed a glory to Moses that was beyond simply seeing a physical manifestation of a human body (like God used to speak with Abraham). Moses saw a manifestation of light and a shape of a body that was a greater glory than the appearance of a man, but Moses did not see the spirit appearance of Almighty God.

Returning to the story of Abraham, the scripture makes it clear that it was the ETERNAL who spoke to him. Again, God did this by making a physical body appear before Abraham through which God spoke. This physical body was not God. Once God was finished with His visit with Abraham, the physical body through which He manifested Himself no longer existed.

After Jesus Christ died and was resurrected, He appeared to some of his disciples on different occasions. At one point, He appeared to the disciples in a room that was completely closed (Luke 24 and John 20). After being resurrected, He was fully spirit and no longer human in a physical body. Christ was in a spirit body. Yet, even in this, Jesus Christ chose to manifest Himself as he appeared when He was in His physical body, but now with the wounds in His side, feet and hands.

Indeed, if God so chooses, He can make a physical body appear before others and communicate to them through that body; but that body is not God.

The Mystery of Melchizedek
Melchizedek is known as being a high priest of God unto Abraham. In the book of Hebrews, Jesus Christ is spoken of as being made a High Priest after the order of Melchizedek. First,

let's notice what the Book of Hebrews has to say concerning Melchizedek:

> *For this Melchizedek, king of Salem, priest of the most high God, who met Abraham returning from the slaughter of the kings, blessed him, to whom also Abraham gave a tenth part of all* (tithe), *and who first being by interpretation King of righteousness, and after that also King of Salem, which is, King of peace, and being without father, without mother, without descent, and having neither beginning of days, nor end of life, but **made like** [Gk.–"modeled after, to copy like, to produce a facsimile, to render similar"] unto the Son of God, now **continually** [forever] **abides** a priest.* (Hebrews 7:1-3)

This story of Melchizedek is introduced on an occasion when Abram (whose name God later changed to Abraham) went to rescue his nephew, Lot, who had been taken captive by invading kings (Genesis 14). At this point, Melchizedek met Abram as he was returning from the victory he had over the kings. Lot returned with Abram, along with all the people and goods that had been taken away. It says that Melchizedek met Abram and blessed him, and that Abram paid his tithes to Melchizedek.

The story is very general in nature, but Paul used it to teach some very important lessons to the Hebrews concerning the importance of Jesus Christ, who was now the High Priest of God forever, after the order of Melchizedek.

The story is important for reasons other than what Paul addressed. As it says in Hebrews 7, this Melchizedek was without father, without mother and without descent. He was a man in physical appearance, but it is clear he was not born of mankind, since he had no father or mother, and he had no lineage of mankind. Some have speculated he may have been an angel or even Jesus Christ, but neither is true.

It states that this Melchizedek had "neither beginning of days, nor end of life." Angels were created, and therefore, they had a beginning. Jesus Christ died and was placed in the tomb for three days and three nights, so certainly He had an "end of life," and, as we have already covered, He did not have life until He was born of His mother, Mary.

It should be easy to understand who Melchizedek was. There is only one being that has never had a beginning of days or an end of life, and since this is the definition of eternal life, then Melchizedek could only be the ETERNAL God. But how is this possible?

This is similar to what we read earlier, where God manifested a human body for Abraham to see, through which God then visited with him. Melchizedek was another means through which God worked with Abraham, and Melchizedek was a representation of what Jesus Christ would become.

Rather than speaking directly to Abraham through a physically manifested body, God worked through a physically manifested man who was presented to others as the priest of God. Abraham's attitude and respect toward a physical appearing priest of God was an important part of Abraham's training and testing. Abraham regarded Melchizedek with the honor he should have shown a representative of God, but in this case, it was God who was working directly with him. Again, this physical manifestation of Melchizedek could not contain the ETERNAL God, but God did work through this Melchizedek to further accomplish His work with Abraham, through whom He (God) would bring about great things in His plan.

Hebrews 7:3 states that this Melchizedek was modeled after the likeness of what Jesus Christ would become. At the time of Abraham, there was no one who would continually abide as God's high priest in direct service to Him, but since the resurrection of Jesus Christ, there is one who will continually abide before God as High Priest—His very Son!

Melchizedek functioned only as God lived through him. Melchizedek was not a separate individual living being, but only a vessel through whom God worked. Melchizedek functioned (in physical appearance as a priest) as a representative of God. Notice what is said of Christ who became High Priest:

> *So also, Christ did not glorify Himself to be made a high priest, but He who said to Him, "You are My Son, today have I begotten you," and as He said also in another place, "You are a priest for ever after the order of Melchizedek."* (Hebrews 5:5-6)

It would be good to notice from where both of these scriptures were quoted.

The first quote is from a Psalm that is a prophecy about something that Christ would later declare:

> *"I will declare the decree," the* **ETERNAL ONE** [Yahweh] *has said to Me, "You are My Son, and this day have I begotten you."* (Psalms 2:7).

The second quote is a prophecy David wrote concerning Jesus Christ:

> *The ETERNAL ONE* [Yahweh] *has sworn, and will not change, "You* [the Messiah] *are a priest forever after the order* [Heb.–manner] *of Melchizedek."* (Psalms 110:4)

Jesus Christ has become God's High Priest forever, and He will continually abide in this office for mankind.

Mankind to Become the God-kind

God's entire purpose for all creation (everything He created) is to reproduce Himself by bringing into existence a God Family (Elohim). From the beginning there has only been the ETERNAL (Yahweh) who is God (El), the Almighty Creator, and there was no one else!

God first created the angelic realm within the spirit world. They were created first, and they were the first to share in His great plan and purpose. The angels were created as spirit beings for the purpose of caring for God's physical creation and serving Him to give help and assistance to those whom God would bring into Elohim. When Paul was speaking of the greatness of God's Son, he also spoke of the purpose for the creation of the angels:

> *Are they* [the angels] *not all ministering* [serving] *spirits, who are sent forth as ministers* [as servants] *for them who shall become heirs of salvation?* (Hebrews 1:14)

Then God created the physical universe. He did this for His great plan that would extend into the millions of years beyond the time of physical mankind. After a long period of time (possibly multiple millions of earth years), God finally came to the point where He created man. He focused His great plan upon the earth, for it would be on the earth, in all the vastness of His physical universe, that God would begin His greatest phase of all creation.

God created the first man on the earth on a physical plane (purely physical), but man was created in the image and likeness of God Himself. However, God said that His purpose was for man to be created in His image and likeness on a spiritual plane. Mankind can never become of the greatness and power of Almighty God, but he can become spirit, on a God plane, in the God Family.

All of this is why the story of Hebrews 2 (quoting David in Psalms 8) is so incredible:

When I consider Your heavens, and the work of Your fingers, and the moon and the stars, which You have ordained, what is man that You are mindful of him, and the son of man that you visit him? For You have made him a little [a little while] *lower than the angels, and have crowned him with glory and honor. You made him to have dominion over the works of Your hands, and You have put all things under his feet.* (Psalms 8:3-6)

Indeed, God's purpose is to put all things under the feet (under the control) of mankind, once mankind has fully become the God-kind, in Elohim (the Family of God). In Hebrews 2, Paul quotes from David and goes on to say that we **do not <u>yet</u>** see all things put under mankind, but we do see that all things have now come under Jesus Christ. Paul stated this thirty years after Jesus Christ died and was resurrected into the God Family. At this moment in time, Paul was showing that all things put under the feet of mankind were only evident in the life of Jesus Christ. The point being, that in time, through Jesus Christ, all mankind will have the opportunity to enter Elohim, just as He (Jesus Christ) did as the firstborn into the Kingdom of God, and then (when man enters Elohim) all things will be under his feet as well.

The greatest miracle that God can perform is that of transforming the mind of man into oneness and unity with Himself so that man can become of the God-kind. This process began first in His only begotten Son, so that through Him (Jesus Christ) the rest of mankind could begin this process of change. The first step in this change is accomplished by being forgiven of sin through our Passover. Then, when sin is not present (has been forgiven), God and His Son can dwell in us to bring about a change in our thinking.

Mankind by nature resists God. When God created all He did, it came into being instantly and nothing resisted Him. However, man resists God because of his carnal nature, and that nature must be changed through a transformation of the mind (of man's thinking). Mankind must go through this process in order for him to genuinely have free choice of God's true ways.

In an instant, all creation came into being when God commanded it, but mankind being transformed into Elohim is not something that can be created instantly by God's command. Man has the choice, once it is given to him in God's perfect timing, to decide for himself if he truly wants God's ways. This process of choice and change (transformation of the mind) takes a lifetime to accomplish. Holy, righteous character is not something that can be commanded to exist. It cannot be accomplished instantly, not even in days and months; it takes years for the process to become complete.

That which has been addressed in this last section is a summary of what was covered in this chapter concerning the ETERNAL God's (Yahweh Elohim's) plan and purpose for His Family. His Family will be born of mankind after mankind has been begotten spiritually and the mind of man has been transformed from selfish, carnal nature to oneness and agreement with God's holy, righteous nature. This can be accomplished only by each individual's willing free choice. The God-kind will be born out of mankind only after mankind has been begotten of God's holy spirit and has grown to the point of maturity where the mind of man can be born of spirit.

This is the process that traditional Christianity confuses with the Biblical term being "born again." The world of traditional Christianity believes that being "born again" is something that people experience when they "give their heart to the Lord." They use such religious sounding platitudes as a "show" of their pseudo-conversion. Being "born again" is about being begotten spiritually and the spiritual growth that follows until the time one can actually be truly born again. Such birth is a spiritual birth into a spirit body—into Elohim. This is the very thing Jesus Christ told Nicodemus:

> *Except a man be born again, he cannot see the kingdom of God* [Elohim] . . . *That which is born of the flesh is flesh, and that which is born of the spirit is spirit.* (John 3:3, 6)

Mankind is born of mankind and is flesh (physical), but anyone who is born of God, into His Family, is spirit.

The TRUE God of Abraham

Do you believe what you have read? If you do not yet believe all that is written in this book, in time, God will make certain that you do know it! It may not be in this age of man. The entire story of God's plan and purpose for His Family and why man's age must now be brought to a close is the story of this book. It is **all** true, and it is from the God of Abraham to you!

If you believe anything about God other than what is written in this book, then you do not know the **true** God of Abraham. This book reveals God's plan and purpose being worked out on this earth, and therefore, it reveals the true God!

The world you know is about to change completely. Now is the time for this change, and you simply happen to be living at this special time in all earth's history. It is the most momentous time in man's history.

Aside from the time of Noah's flood, man, as a whole, has been able to continue through the normal cycles of life, choosing to live life his own way, generation after generation. The time you live in is not such a time. You live at the very end of man's self-rule on earth. It is now time for God's rule to begin.

Only a very small percentage of human life will continue on into that new era that will begin after the return of Jesus Christ as King of kings over all the earth. The luxury of time being on your side, as a normal course of man's existence (as it has been over the past 6,000 years), is about to come to an abrupt end! Time is not on your side any longer. **You have before you true life and death decisions that must be made quickly if you have any hope of sharing in that new age.**

When this book is published at the end of summer of 2006, (with distribution in full swing in the fall), there will be a maximum time of two years remaining before the world will be plunged into the worst time of all human history.

By the fall of 2008, the United States will have collapsed as a world power, or it will have begun its collapse and no longer exist as an independent nation within six months after that time. There is a marginal, six-month window of time that God has not yet revealed concerning this specific moment of time. This will be revealed some time soon after the distribution of this book begins.

As the spokesman of God's two end-time witnesses and as His end-time prophet, I have fulfilled my responsibility in placing the contents of this book before you. What you do with it is up to you. Indeed, only a very short time remains before it will be evident that I am who I say or that I am not. In the past 1900 years, have you ever read or heard of a publication from any religious leader who has made such claims, laying out such a precise pattern for the near future with such precise timelines? You have not! This is the evidence (witness, testimony) of the true God of Abraham!